Computer Security Policies and SunScreen™ Firewalls

Kathryn M. Walker
Linda Croswhite Cavanaugh

Sun Microsystems Press
A Prentice Hall Title

The publisher offers discounts on this book when ordered in bulk quantities.
For more information, contact Corporate Sales Department, Prentice Hall PTR ,
One Lake Street, Upper Saddle River, NJ 07458. Phone: 800-382-3419; FAX: 201- 236-7141.
E-mail: corpsales@prenhall.com.

Editorial/production supervision: *Maria Molinari*
Cover design director: *Jerry Votta*
Cover designer: *Scott Weiss*
Manufacturing manager: *Alexis R. Heydt*
Marketing manager: *Kaylie Smith*
Acquisitions editor: *Gregory G. Doench*
SunSoft Press publisher: *Rachel Borden*

10 9 8 7 6 5 4 3 2 1

ISBN 0-13-096015-2

Sun Microsystems Press
A Prentice Hall Title

Contents

≡

Figures

Tables

Acknowledgments

The authors are extremely indebted to many people for help with this book.

We have special thanks for Bill Danielson, Distinguished Engineer at Sun Microsystems, Inc., and architect of the SunScreen firewalls, who contributed many hours of his time both reviewing the manuscript and providing instruction in the areas of security, networking, and firewalls. Bill was involved with this project from the beginning, and gave us needed direction and support in all areas of the book.

Glenn Scott, Director of Engineering and chief technologist in the Internet Commerce and Security Group at Sun Microsystems, Inc., gave us the support and the time to work on this book. Without him, this book would not be a reality.

Many people at Sun Microsystems, Inc., contributed their time and expertise. We are grateful to Sun Microsystems engineers Gene Anaya for his conscientious reviewing that made the book much more complete and technically accurate; Marc Dye for his help in putting together the network security policy example in Chapter 6; and Christopher Kampmeier, who provided excellent review comments, and also helped develop the material for the firewall scenarios. Martyn N. Perry, Lead Technical Writer for the SunScreen products, reviewed the entire manuscript, providing valuable technical and editorial comments. We want to thank all the members of the SunScreen and SKIP teams, and especially those who provided manuscript review and valuable input: David Ballman, Gary Wolfe, Mary Artibee, Andre Lewis, Rich Skrenta, Frank DeMarco, Anthony Scarpino, Tom Markson, and Bryn Dole.

We acknowledge and thank Harvey B. Castro, Information Security Consultant, for manuscript review and his important contributions, especially to the security policy discussion in Chapter 1.

Thanks to Rachel Borden and John Bortner of Sun Microsystems Press, and Greg Doench at Prentice Hall, for their professionalism, support, and good humor seeing this book through from inception to publication. And thank you to our editors, Mary Lou Nohr, Lisa Iarkowski, and Maria Molinari.

Finally, some notes of personal thanks.

Kathryn M. Walker thanks her manager, Linda Cavanaugh, for believing in this book, and for giving me the support and the time to write it. I am forever grateful to my father, my mother, and my friends for their encouragement in helping me realize a lifelong goal of writing and publishing a book. I am also very grateful to Suzanne Chapple at Sun Microsystems, Inc., the earliest supporter for my idea of writing a book on security, and Vipin Samar, who helped me get started in the security area and was also an early proponent for a book on security.

Linda Croswhite Cavanaugh would like to thank Kathryn Walker for allowing me to be part of this book, and for reminding me when my dates were near. I would also like to thank my husband for his loving support, and especially for taking care of our baby so I could write. Without my mother's early support and belief in me, I may never have chosen a writing career. Thanks, Mom. Finally, there are many people in my life, both past and present, that have contributed to my becoming a writer. I thank you all.

May 1, 1998, Palo Alto, California

       Kathryn M. Walker (walkerkm@acm.org)

       Linda Croswhite Cavanaugh (lindac@acm.org)

Preface

This Book's Focus

Computer Security Policies and SunScreen Firewalls focuses on the development of security policies and how the SunScreen™ EFS™ and the SunScreen™ SPF-200 firewall products can be used to implement security policies.

This book focuses mainly on information protection as a reason for establishing a security policy, and on protecting information against electronic threats from outside an organization or from inside an organization. As such, it is concerned primarily with network security, rather than other aspects of security, such as physical security.

Who Should Read This Book

The intended audience for this book includes IS or IT managers, network planners, MIS managers, system administrators, and anyone involved with planning or implementing a security policy.

This book assumes a working knowledge of networking and UNIX®. No specific background in security is required.

How This Book Is Organized

This book contains the following chapters and appendices:

- Chapter 1, "What Is a Security Policy?"

- Chapter 2, "Firewalls as Part of Your Security Strategy"
- Chapter 3, "Security Concepts and the Technology Behind Them"
- Chapter 4, "How the SunScreen Firewalls Work"
- Chapter 5, "Managing SunScreen Firewalls"
- Chapter 6, "Translating Your Security Policy to Your SunScreen Firewalls"
- Appendix A, "Scenarios with the SunScreen EFS Firewall"
- Appendix B, "Resources"

References to the SunScreen product in this book apply to both the SunScreen EFS and SPF-200 products, unless stated otherwise.

For purposes of this book, there are no differences between the domestic or export versions of the SunScreen products, that is, everything discussed in this book can be done with a global version and with an export-controlled version of the product, unless specifically stated otherwise.

What Is a Security Policy? 1 ≡

The Need for Security

An organization, whether it is a commercial business, an educational facility, a government agency, or any other type, needs to protect (secure) its information, its resources, and its reputation from potential threats, actual misuse, or accidental misuse. Information, resources, and reputation are part of an organization's *assets*; if they are compromised, harm could result to the organization.

There are various areas of security, such as physical security, personnel security, and computer and network (electronic) security. This book focuses on computer and network security.

What Is a Threat?

Computer threats and actual computer "attacks" have been extensively documented in newspapers, news and computer trade magazines, books, on various Internet sites, on television, and elsewhere. Over the last few years, the number of these threats has grown, and the number of organizations affected has also grown. Attacks can come from someone inside or outside an organization. Attacks can be intentional or unintentional.

As an example, in March 1998, the Computer Security Institute in San Francisco, California, reported in its third annual "Computer Crime and Security Survey" that 64% of its 520 respondents (from government, financial, educational, and corporate sites) reported computer security breaches within the last twelve months. That figure is a 16% increase over the previous year's survey. Acknowledged financial losses from those security breaches were up 36% from 1997, totaling over $136,000,000 (for those able to quantify their losses). The biggest financial losses occurred through unauthorized access by insiders. Another significant finding of the survey is that the number of respondents reporting their Internet connection as a point of attack grew from 47% in 1997 to 54% in 1998.[1]

Examples of Computer Threats

What does it mean to talk about threats to an organization's security:

- on the Internet? (a network outside your organization)
- on the intranet? (a network inside your organization)

An organization's assets are immediately at risk when it chooses to connect to the Internet. It might want to connect to the Internet so that it can provide services to its employees, as well as access to certain information. It might also want to provide Internet services for its customers and other users of the Internet.

There are different types of threats that result in varying degrees of losses. Some examples include service interruption, whereby an attacker shuts down a network service to the outside world; theft of online proprietary information or interception of sensitive electronic mail or data as it is transmitted; and fraudulent misrepresentation of either data or someone as a user.

Thus, you may want to restrict access from the outside to your organization's network. You may also want to isolate certain networks within your organization to protect information. For example, you may want to confine all financial records to one particular network and restrict access to that network to those authorized to see the financial records.

The Importance of a Security Policy

The *need to protect* an organization's assets results in the need for a security policy.

---

1. See http://www.gocsi.com for the complete report.

A security policy is, in general, the total of all of an organization's procedures and rules related to security. A security policy should establish an organization-wide program of how both internal and external users interact with an organization's computer network, how the overall computer architecture topology will be implemented, and where computer assets will be located. But a security policy needs to be more than that. It must be a comprehensive, well-thought-out, and tested plan for the entire organization, with procedures that are constantly tested and updated as the organization's needs change and as security issues change. As technology changes and the kinds of security threats change, the policy must be adaptable. A security policy should be written to *anticipate* problems, as well as address known problems.

Why a Security Policy?

Security policies will vary by organization. There is no one "best" policy for everyone because organizations are unique; each organization has its own purposes, goals, and business interests. For example, a military base has different security concerns from those of a company doing business over the Internet; a company doing business over the Internet has different security concerns from those of a university.

This does not mean that guidelines for policies are not helpful. A general "template" for a policy can be useful when you are beginning to develop a security policy; it will, however, have to be adapted to the particular organization and its particular goals and management direction.

There are various reasons to establish a security policy. The basic motivation is the need to protect an organization's assets. Some of the more common reasons are:

- Legal.
  Depending on your organization's purpose or business, there may be legal requirements that require you to define certain aspects of your organization's activities. An example of this could be in the health care industry, where there is a need to keep patient records confidential. Privacy laws pertinent to your organization may require you to maintain a security policy.

- Regulatory.

  There may be government or industry regulations directly affecting your organization that require specifying how data is handled. This requirement could be applicable for financial institutions, for example.

- Contractual.

  Contracts with governments may contain security-related requirements, such as information classification. Often, the approach to these requirements can be spelled out in a security policy.[1]

- Information protection.

  Protecting data, or information, from disclosure or modification is critical. This protection extends to information such as your organization's proprietary information, business plans, information about your customers, information that could potentially cause damage to your organization's reputation, and so forth.

- The welfare of the organization.

  The ability of an organization to continue to function and to carry out its goals and objectives is a basic need.

Good security starts with a security policy.

This book focuses mainly on protecting information that exists on a computer or is conveyed electronically as the main reason for establishing a security policy. It does not cover, for example, protecting the spoken word or protecting material printed in hard-copy documents. However, much of the discussion in this chapter is applicable to developing any security policy, regardless of the primary motivation for having a policy.

Who Writes a Security Policy?

As a general rule, security policies are written by someone at a fairly high level in the organization's structure, such as a Security Officer, Information Officer, or others in an Information Security (IS) or Information Technology (IT) group. A group with a similar title or charter for a security policy may or may not

---

1. The United States Department of Defense defines its recognized levels of computer security in a document *Trusted Computer Standards Evaluation Criteria*, also known as the Orange Book.

exist when you begin to develop a foundation for your security policy. If it does not already exist, the creation of such a group may be part of the overall proposal to senior management regarding security.

Although the security policy may be written by one person, such as an Information Officer, other groups within an organization must be involved in the development and implementation of the policy. These groups most likely should include Human Resources, the Legal department, Audit, and the technical staff (including system administrators, operators, etc.). There may be others groups that should be involved; again, this depends on your particular organization.

Policy creation must be a joint effort by a representative group of decision makers, technical personnel, and day-to-day users from different levels within the organization. Decision makers must have the power to enforce the policy, technical personnel will advise on the ramifications of the policy, and day-to-day users will have a say in how "usable" the policy is.

Senior management support and approval is very important. A justification for spending time, resources, and money on security should include an analysis of the value of information to be protected versus the estimate of damage to the organization if the information is compromised.

Starting Out

Some basic questions to ask about your organization are "Against what or whom am I trying to protect my organization?" "What is the cost of an *insecure* network?" "What is the cost of protecting information?" Or, "What do I have to lose?" Or, "What does it cost *not* to have a security policy?" The answers to these questions will help you start to build a foundation for your policy and develop a risk analysis.

The more you understand your business needs ("business" in the sense of your organization's overall purpose or goals, not just commercial goals), the more you can understand your security needs. Security should not be viewed as an isolated and unrelated endeavor; it should be viewed as *part* of your organization's business.

The policy will weigh possible threats and security priorities against the value of personal productivity and the organization's assets, which need different levels of protection. The policy will define the organization's expectations of computer and network use and define procedures to prevent and respond to security incidents.

Figure 1-1 gives a guideline for the steps for preparing and maintaining a security policy. These steps are discussed further in this chapter.

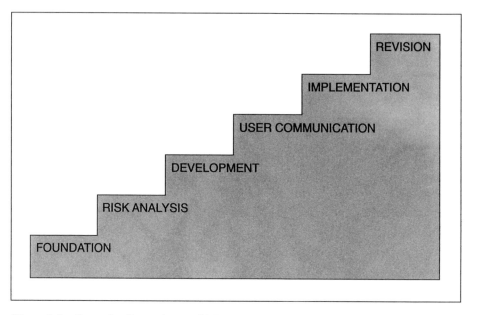

Figure 1-1   Steps for Preparing and Maintaining a Security Policy

Building a Foundation for the Policy

A security policy needs a solid foundation. Building a foundation involves conducting research, analyzing information, and getting consensus. The foundation should include a sound understanding of answers to questions such as:

- Against what or whom am I trying to protect the organization?
- What do we want to accomplish in this policy? What are our security objectives?
- What items should go into the policy?

- What approvals are needed?
- Who is involved?
- What are the business requirements of the organization?
- What is the management direction for the organization?

It is important to recognize that information is an asset. This recognition is a basic motivation for the policy. As an asset, information needs to be protected to ensure its integrity, confidentiality, and availability.

Identify the Organization's Assets

Create a list of all the items that need to be protected, the location, and the owner. When considering information to be protected, consider data stored in various locations, such as online, archived offline, in backups, in audit logs, and in databases, as well as data while it is being executed, and data in transit over networks.

Develop a Mission Statement

A mission statement is a brief explanation of your overall goals. A mission statement is particularly helpful if you are just beginning to develop a security policy and have nothing in place; it will help focus your policy. A mission statement could also list responsibilities.

Example

Information is a key asset of the company. Recognizing this, the goal of the Corporate Information Security (IS) Group is to protect information from being compromised in any way. The IS group will do this through the development and implementation of security policies and procedures, which will be applicable to the whole company.

Develop a Draft Budget

You need to factor in costs for time and people who will be involved in developing and implementing the security policy. Also include the cost of any hardware or software you are recommending for purchase to help with risk analysis or to help implement the security policy, for example, a firewall. Remember to include items such as a contractor's time, if appropriate.

1

Enlist Management Support

Support from your organization's senior management is extremely important to the success of the security policy. For a security policy to be approved and enforced, it must have the backing of senior management. Authorization, funding for resources, and other critical elements in an overall security strategy may need approval from senior management.

When seeking management support, it can be helpful to specifically address the reality of security issues and directly relate these to the business issues of your organization. A risk analysis is useful (risk analysis is discussed in the next section). You should prepare a cost justification in advance. You could also highlight any legal, regulatory, and audit requirements.

Allot Sufficient Time

Foundations for security policies take time to develop. You should expect to spend at minimum one month to develop your security policy foundation.

Analyzing Risks

Risk analysis is a process of examining all of your risks or threats, ranking those risks by a level of severity, and making cost-effective decisions on what you want to protect.

What types of problems could potentially result from a security problem? Some possible risks to your network include:

- Unauthorized access
- Unavailable service, which can include some or all network services, corruption of data, or a slowdown due to a virus; the result can be downtime and lost productivity
- Disclosure of sensitive information, such as to a competitor, or theft of information, such as credit card information; damage from data being used by the perpetrator
- Lost data
- Corrupted data
- Loss of confidence in the security of your data
- Cost to replace stolen or destroyed data
- Cost to fix the problem

Develop your risk analysis keeping in mind possible threats from people within your organization as well as risks from people on computer networks outside your organization.

Once you have a list of risks, you should develop a strategy or some formula for weighing the risk against the importance of the resource. This strategy will help to determine how much effort should be spent protecting the resource.[1]

A security policy needs to strike the best balance for your organization between protection and productivity. There is almost always a balance that has to be worked out; complete security (if such a thing were possible) could mean bringing any meaningful work to a halt.

Assess the money and time potentially to be spent on network security versus the damage that could result from a security problem. Any countermeasures that you put in place should be measurable.

Developing the Security Policy

Once you have built your foundation for the security policy, identified threats, and done a risk analysis, you are ready to develop the security policy; the security policy will identify how you are going to mitigate the risks.

Structure: Policies, Standards, Procedures

Policies, standards, and procedures are terms often used when describing areas of security. They are sometimes used interchangeably, but for purposes of this discussion, they each have their own meaning.

A *policy* is a broad, high-level statement that describes management's objectives. It answers a "what?" question, for example, "What do we want to accomplish?" or "What rules do we want to operate under?" A *standard* is a more specific statement than a policy; it answers the question "how?" A *procedure* shows step by step how to do a task; it answers the question "in

---

1. One possible formula is to put a figure on the probability of a threat happening, estimate the loss from that threat (usually in a dollar amount), and multiply those two figures. With this formula, you can now better identify the countermeasures to take; for example, if your risk is $100,000, determine whether it is worth it to spend $250,000 on the secure solution.

detail, how?" Security policies sometimes also include guidelines; a *guideline* is a suggestion or recommendation about how to do something; it is not a requirement.

Figure 1-2 illustrates this hierarchy.

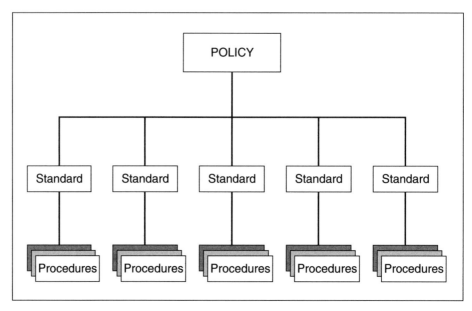

Figure 1-2   Hierarchy of Policies, Standards, and Procedures

Example

Policy: The security policy discusses the importance of information protection. A number of standards and services are referenced; one item is the backup of data.

Standard: A number of standards are referred to by the policy, including a standard for backups. The standard for backups includes definitions for various types of backups, the schedule for backups, where backup copies are kept offsite, and so on.

Procedure: One of the procedures documented under the standard for backups is how to use the UNIX `cron` utility.

In terms of structure, there can be one high-level, "umbrella" policy that references standards but does not give specifics about them; the standards and the procedures contain the details. A high-level policy could also create a foundation for subpolicies that in turn reference standards, if you decide to organize information that way. Again, there is no one way to write a security policy. You seek a balance between how much detail versus general information to include and how to structure that information.

Place technical standards and details in the technical standards sections of your security policy. This type of structure makes maintenance of the policy much easier. Technology changes quickly, and with this arrangement you don't need to update your top-level security policy every time a technical detail changes; you need only update your standards or procedures. In addition, every time you change a standard or a procedure, you won't need to go through a complete approval process again.

Although a security policy is usually written by a security officer or other high-level person, standards and procedures are usually written by technical people, such as system administrators and computer operators, who have the technical knowledge. The policy can reference standards, for example, a standard for backups; a member of the technical staff would then support the security officer by writing the standard.

Include everything that needs to be said; don't omit something from the policy because you think it may be too obvious.

It is not necessary to write all policies, standards, and procedures at the same time. You can establish priorities based on your organization's needs or the severity of the risks involved.

The security policy developed must conform to existing organization policies, rules, regulations, and laws that the organization is subject to. Any applicable policies should be identified and taken into consideration while developing the security policy.

Some Suggested Topics for Standards

Part of setting up your security policy includes defining standards and services that will be available, for both internal and external users.

Examples of some standards you might address in your policy include:

- Information classification

  This section could describe how various kinds of information should be classified, for example, Proprietary, Confidential, and so on.

- Access controls

  Who needs to be able to log in remotely from other locations? What are the login procedures?

- Employee terminations

  This section might describe the process for notifying an employee of termination, what actions must be taken, by whom, the time frame, and so on.

- Internet or network services, such as telnet, FTP, and HTTP

  To what services do employees need access? For example, do users need to transfer files outside the organization? Do they need to download files from outside the organization?

  You may want to consider whether you are primarily trying to protect your organization from the outside or from the inside. It is easier to block people trying to gain access from the outside because you know what services to block. One way to look at this situation is that you trust your internal users to do what they say they are doing; for example, if a user says he is using telnet, he really is just using telnet, and not using telnet to hide some other activity.

  Connections coming in involve services over which you have control. So one of the basic questions to ask is, "What services do I need to allow to the outside?"

- Electronic mail (email)

- Contractor versus employee resource use

- Virus protection

- Backup standards

- Emergency and contingency standards

- Passwords

Considering Tools and Technology

Various tools and technologies are available to assist in implementing security policies. Firewalls are one example. It is useful to do some research into the technology available and evaluate it according to your needs before making a recommendation to management. It is advisable to have at least one proposed solution ready when presenting a security policy and strategy to management.

This book does not address all the various technologies available; it concentrates on firewalls, and in particular, the SunScreen firewalls, as a technology to implement security policies.

Security Policy Components

A security policy should contain these sections:

Statement of Purpose

This section should be a brief statement of why the policy was developed and what is to be protected, or "Here's why we need this policy."

Scope

This section should include a discussion of the policy's applicability. If your organization is spread over geographical areas or is international, you could explain in detail here which divisions, business units, geographical areas, countries, etc., the policy applies to.

This section might also include an explanation of the types of information, definitions, and what is covered under the policy.

The scope section could also describe the technical platforms that the policy applies to, according to operating system or hardware platform, for example.

Policy Statement

The policy statement should describe who is responsible for the policy, including roles and responsibilities. For example, part of a policy statement might read "The System Administrator is responsible for administering the backup and recovery procedures."

The roles and responsibilities should also include a statement of who is going to monitor for compliance to the security policy. The role of monitoring for compliance and the role of enforcement are two different functions. Usually, monitoring for compliance is done by an IS group or internal audit group that reports any violations to management; enforcement is usually done by management.

The policy statement may also contain a description of the rules that you want to implement.

Enforcement

This section specifies who (person or group) is charged with enforcing the security policy. For various reasons, enforcement should be done by management.

Any penalties for noncompliance with the policy can be described here also.

Exceptions

If any exceptions to the security policy can be allowed, describe them here. Also describe the process for requesting an exception.

Additional Considerations

Identifying the date or revised date of the policy and the source of the policy (which person and which department produced it) are useful to document.

Writing Style

When writing the policy, be sure to use language and a writing style that everyone can understand.

Review and Approval Process

The completed policy should go through a review and approval process that ensures that everyone who needs to give input to the policy has had an opportunity to do so. This process will also help ensure that the policy is compliant with other organizational policies or legal requirements.

When the policy is completed, it should be signed by the appropriate people.

Communicating the Policy to Users

The security policy should include a formalized process that communicates the site security policy to all users. In addition, an educational campaign, or "security awareness program," should make users aware of how computer and network systems are expected to be used and how to protect themselves from unauthorized users.

All users should be informed about what is considered the proper use of their account or computer. This information can be communicated easily by giving users a copy of the security policy at the time they get an account. If your organization provides new employees with any handouts, the security policy could be included in that as well.

If your organization maintains an internal web page, this is a good place to put a copy of the policy as well.

The strategy for communicating to users should also take into account how to communicate changes or revisions to the policy.

Everyone is responsible for security.

Implementing the Policy

The method of implementing the policy will vary by organization, depending on the policy itself, the technology used, the organization's needs, and other factors.

Some questions to consider include the following: Will the policy be implemented across the entire organization at once, or by group? If your organization is international, will you implement by geographic area first, or all at once? Will the policy be implemented as a whole, or in parts, according to priority?

Implement and Test Rules

If you are using a SunScreen Firewall product to implement your security policy, you are ready to translate your standards to *rules* for the firewall. This process is described in Chapter 6, "Translating Your Security Policy to Your SunScreen Firewalls."

Test as many of the rules as can conceivably be done. Check to be sure that data is being handled as you have specified in the rules.

Define Emergency Procedures/Response

A response should be in place before any violation or breakdown of security occurs.

Planning responses for different scenarios in advance—without an actual security violation occurring—is good practice. Not only do you need to define actions based on the type of violation, you also need to have a clearly defined series of actions based on the kind of user violating your computer security policy.

When a policy violation has been detected, the immediate course of action should already be defined to ensure prompt and proper enforcement. Audit trails, at least in the form of computer logs, may be required. An investigation should be performed to determine how and why the violation occurred. Then, the appropriate corrective action should be executed. The type and severity of action taken varies depending on the type of violation that occurred.

The response should consider when outside agencies should be notified, and by whom.

After a security incident, a report describing the incident, method of discovery, correction procedure, monitoring procedure, summary of what was learned, and any recommendations for updating the security policy, should be written and distributed to the appropriate people.

Monitor for Compliance

Monitoring for compliance to the policy is usually done with a combination of an information security officer and an internal audit group. It could also be done by an external auditor or consultant. If your organization is in a regulated industry in the U.S., state auditors may be involved.

Reviewing and Updating the Policy

Security policies should be reviewed whenever an organization changes its goals and strategies. Because technology changes quickly, security policies should be reviewed regularly, at least once a year, even if an organization has not changed its goals.

Be proactive about security. Some actions you can take include:

- Keep up with the latest security issues, threats, and information available
- Review your organization's security policies regularly
- Review your organization's systems and networks regularly; ask "How well are things working?"
- Review your organization's assets and business needs regularly
- Read log files routinely, checking for any unusual or suspicious items

Changes and revisions to the policy should go through a review and approval process, and approved changes should be communicated to users.

The next chapter discusses how firewalls can be part of your security strategy.

Firewalls as Part of Your Security Strategy 2≡

What Is a Firewall?

A *firewall* is a system that controls network access between two or more networks. It is located at the point at which one network connects to another network, such as the point between two networks within an organization or the point between an internal network and a public network, such as the Internet. A firewall sits at this point, controlling access into and out of a network. Firewalls are sometimes referred to as *perimeter* defenses.

Figure 2-1 illustrates a sample firewall implementation.

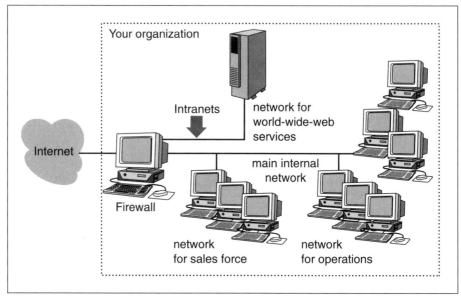

Figure 2-1   Example of a Firewall Implementation

Early computer networks were not designed with security as a priority because it was generally assumed that sites and users connected to the network could, by and large, be trusted. This is no longer a good assumption. In addition to potential threats from *outside* an organization, *internal users* might accidentally or deliberately expose data or services from within an organization to an outside network or user.

On the Internet

The purpose of a firewall is to ensure that all communication between the local organization's network and an external network conforms to the organization's network security policies. An example of a network security policy might be "allow internal user access to all services on the Internet unless expressly denied." Once the security policies and standards are established, a firewall can be used to assist in implementing a network environment based on the established policies.

On the Intranet

Firewall systems can also be deployed within an organization to isolate different servers and networks, in effect controlling access within the network. On the intranet, for example, an organization may want to separate an accounting and payroll server from the rest of the network and allow only certain individuals access to the information on that server.

Thus, firewalls are one method available to implement your organization's security policy or part of the policy.

What Security Problems Does a Firewall Try to Solve?

Firewalls limit exposure by controlling what can be accessed. They provide an authorization mechanism so that only specified users or applications can gain access through the firewall to the network or computers it is protecting.

Firewalls, if so designed, can also provide encryption to protect privacy of data.

In general, firewalls use *packet filtering* to address the problems of access control and authorization.

Packet Filtering

Data that moves on networks is contained in packets. A packet is a unit of data that can be transmitted on a TCP/IP network. IP packets have:

- A source IP address (network number and host number)
- A destination IP address (network number and host number)
- A protocol name (for example, TCP, UDP, ICMP)
- A source port (applies for TCP or UDP only)
- A destination port (applies for TCP or UDP only)

The IP address is used in routing packets. It identifies your host (computer) and your host's location on a network.

The IP addresses are placed with the packet when the packet is created by the program a user is running. The source IP address identifies the host that initiates and sends the packet, and the destination IP address identifies the host that is receiving the packet.[1] When the recipient host responds, that packet has its own IP address as the source IP address, and the original sender's IP address as the destination IP address.

A port number is a *logical* point of contact on a computer. Port numbers are used in TCP and UDP connections to indicate the end points of a connection from a client to a server. The port number on the server is the point of contact used to identify a particular process or service on that server. Ports used in this manner are called *well-known ports*.

Port numbers 0 through 1023 are reserved for well-known port assignments, for example, FTP (port 21), telnet (port 23), SMTP (port 25), gopher (port 70), and World Wide Web HTTP (port 80). These port numbers are assigned by the Internet Assigned Numbers Authority (IANA). The higher ranges of port numbers (port 1024 and above) are used for registered ports and dynamic port number assignments.

Figure 2-2 is a diagram of the Open Systems Interconnection (OSI) model of the seven-layer network. This diagram shows the various layers data passes through as it moves from its source to its destination.

---

1. In the client-server model of computing, the initial sender is the client and the initial receiver is the server.

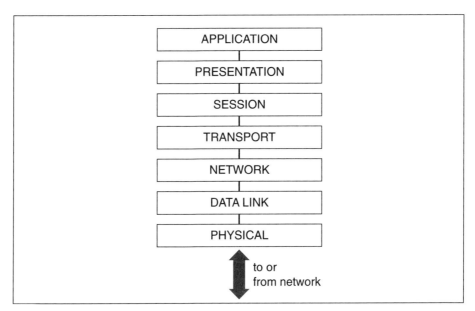

Figure 2-2   OSI Model of Network Protocol Layers

Network protocols are referenced in various places in this book, so it is helpful to have this picture in mind.

In packet filtering, also referred to as packet screening, the firewall sits somewhere on the network between the client and the server and examines each packet as it enters the firewall. Based on information in the packet (such as the IP addresses and port numbers) and a predetermined configuration according to your security policy (in the form of the rules you have defined), the packet is either passed through the firewall or blocked from passing and dropped from the network.

This arrangement enables you to control access to a particular service on a particular address from a particular address. For example, you might allow systems on the Internet to have access only to certain machines, such as your public World Wide Web server. You might further restrict access so systems on the Internet can have access only to web services on those machines and not other potentially more dangerous services, such as telnet. You might allow users on your own network to make TCP connections *out to* services on the Internet, but disallow users on the Internet to make TCP connections *into* your network.

Packet Filtering with State

One problem encountered with traditional packet filtering is that for some protocols it is impossible to determine the services associated with a packet by just looking at that packet. For example, in most UDP protocols, it is impossible for the packet screen to tell whether a packet is a response to a previous request or whether the packet has come from someone pretending to be a response to try to connect to some other service.

Firewalls can solve this problem by keeping *state*. State is the concept of memory of past events. A firewall with state "remembers" enough information about passed packets so that it can correctly determine if a packet should be allowed or denied.

As an example, consider the case where a firewall receives a UDP packet from source port 53 to destination port 2049. Is this UDP packet a response to a DNS request (because the source port is 53, the well-known port for DNS), or is it a request to an NFS® server (because the destination port is 2049, the well-known port for NFS)? If the firewall has state, it remembers whether or not it recently saw a DNS request; thus, it can determine whether the packet is a response to a DNS request or, rather, an NFS request.

State is very good for multimedia connections; the firewall with state monitors commands on an existing connection, and when it sees a command requesting a new multimedia stream from the server, it dynamically allows that stream to pass so that the multimedia program is received correctly by the user.

Packet Filters and Proxies

A firewall is a centralized point of control for data moving between two points (similar to a firewall between two buildings preventing a fire from moving between buildings). Usually, people talk about two networks, an outside network and an inside network. Some people add a third component: a *DMZ*, or demilitarized zone, whose function is to act as a sort of neutral area between the outside and the inside network. Regardless of the components, if you want to control access between two areas, find the point on your network through which all the traffic has to pass; this is known as the *choke point*. If you control data at this one centralized point by putting in a firewall, you don't have to control it at various points.

After you decide on a location for a firewall, you make decisions about where to examine a packet, that is, at which layer in the network protocol stack. Packet filters examine packets at or below the transport layer, or TCP layer. Because of this, it is difficult to examine data at higher layers, such as the application layer. So, for some situations, the concept of a *proxy* is introduced. A proxy examines packets at the application layer.

Figure 2-3 illustrates a client connecting to a server, using only a packet filter to control access. Note that a single TCP connection goes all the way from the client to the server.

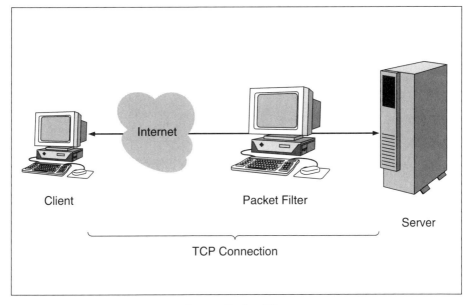

Figure 2-3   A TCP Connection Using a Packet Filter

Figure 2-4 illustrates the TCP connection created when you add a proxy. A proxy can reside on the same machine as the packet filter, or it can reside on a different machine, as shown in Figure 2-4. Note that the original TCP connection from the client stops at the proxy, and the proxy originates a second TCP connection to the server.

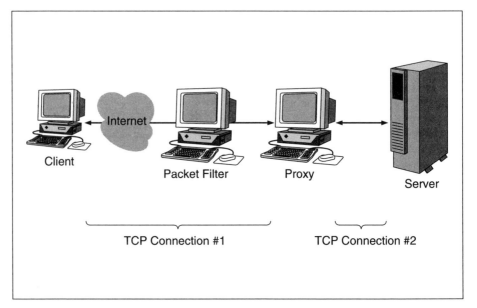

Figure 2-4   Adding a Proxy to a Packet Filter System

Because of this second TCP connection, a proxy is useful as a known "buffer" between outside applications and internal applications on internal servers. A proxy is also useful if you process a lot of data at the application level.

A disadvantage of a proxy strategy is that there is more processing on the firewall; also, there is the overhead of having two TCP connections instead of one connection.

Cryptography

There are benefits from adding cryptographic capability to a packet-screening firewall. With packet screening, you are using IP addresses to control access, and someone can forge an IP address. Cryptography enables you to strongly authenticate the system sending the IP packets, so you do not need to rely only on the IP addresses to control access.

Also, it is possible for people to read data while it is being transmitted, for example, by using a wiretap. If you use cryptography to encrypt your data, you address this situation by adding privacy to your communication.

The concepts related to cryptography and encryption are described in more detail in Chapter 3, "Security Concepts and the Technology Behind Them."

Tunnel Addresses and Network Address Translation

Sometimes, when sending communications, you may want to hide the actual source and destination addresses of packets. *Tunneling* is a concept that allows you to put the original packet into another packet that has a different set of addresses, thereby hiding the original addresses in the packet. The different set of addresses (tunnel addresses) are usually the two firewalls at either end of the "tunnel." Anyone intercepting a communication with tunnel addresses sees only the tunnel addresses of the firewalls, not the internal network's actual source and destination addresses.

Tunneling is usually used with packets that are encrypted. When tunneling and encryption are used together, the result is a *virtual private network* (VPN). A VPN simulates a private connection between two firewalls; the connection is virtual because it is using the Internet, and private because it is using encryption.

Network address translation (NAT) converts internal, or private, IP addresses in your organization to a different set of public IP addresses. This conversion provides some additional protection of your internal network, since attackers cannot see the internal IP addresses of hosts.[1] It solves a problem for those people who didn't formally register internal host IP addresses; they can convert the "made-up," unregistered internal IP addresses to registered IP address for the Internet. A further benefit of using NAT can occur if an organization changes its Internet service provider (ISP) and receives new IP addresses; in this situation, the organization could just remap its existing IP addresses (using NAT) to the new IP addresses from the ISP.

Thus, both tunneling and NAT hide, or mask, internal IP addresses of a machine communicating through a firewall. NAT's primary function, however, is to provide public, registered addresses for communication with external hosts on public networks.

---

1. Although NAT can provide some additional protection by hiding internal addresses, using NAT puts only one additional difficulty in the path of someone trying to get into your network. This approach is sometimes referred to as "security through obscurity." NAT should never be relied on as the only method of security.

SunScreen Firewalls as Part of Your Security

SunScreen EFS and SunScreen SPF-200 are firewall products that you can use to implement the access control and encryption areas of your security policy.

After you have developed your security policy, you translate, or map, the policy into *rules* for your SunScreen products. This process is shown in Figure 2-5. These rules will control services and addresses allowed to pass through the firewall.

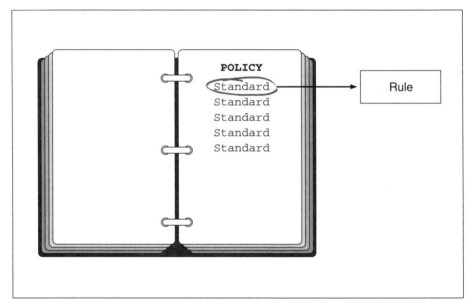

Figure 2-5 Translating Policy Standards to Rules

Example

You may have a standard for the File Transfer Protocol (FTP) written in your security policy. That standard describes under what circumstances and by whom FTP can be used, both from inside and from outside your organization. You will write that FTP standard as a rule (or several rules, depending on how your network is set up) that directs the SunScreen firewall to filter ftp traffic according to what your standard specifies.

When you have your standards written, you are ready to translate the policy into rules for your SunScreen product, as shown in Figure 2-6. The process for translating the policy into rules, and relevant information on cryptography and SunScreen administration, are described in the rest of this book.

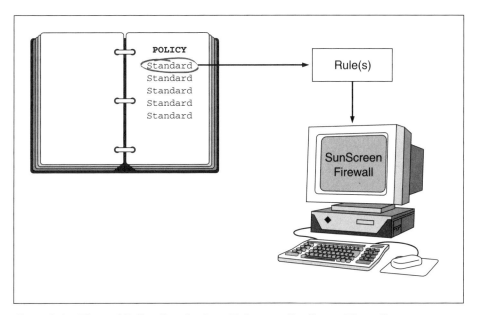

Figure 2-6 Flow of Policy Standards to Rules to a SunScreen Firewall

Security Concepts and the Technology Behind Them   3 ≣

This chapter contains an introductory discussion of security concepts in the context of computers or networks; these concepts are referred to again later in this book. Different kinds of security technologies are available to implement these concepts; this chapter focuses on cryptography, an integral part of the SunScreen firewall products.

Discussion of Some Security Concepts

Authentication, access control, privacy, and integrity are security concepts that are important to understand.

Authentication

Authentication is knowing that someone is actually who he or she claims to be. When using resources or sending messages in a large private network, not to mention the Internet, ascertaining the true identity of users is extremely important.

Authentication refers to the network security service that provides assurance to the receiver of a digital message that it indeed comes from the indicated sender. In the case of a single message, this means that the recipient is assured that the message comes from the source it claims to be from. Authentication prevents a third party from masquerading as one of the two original, legitimate parties.

Example

Cryptography is an example of technology that can provide authentication.

Access Control

After you authenticate someone, access control (sometimes called authorization) is used to limit and control who uses your host systems and applications through your communications links. Each entity—host, network, or nomadic system—with which you communicate over your network must be identified or authenticated so that access to your system is controlled. Once communication is established, data may be exchanged unencrypted or encrypted.

Example

A firewall is an example of technology that can provide access control; the rules control access to network services. Other examples of access control are the standard UNIX file permissions provided in the Solaris™ operating environment.

Privacy

Privacy means ensuring that data or communication is protected so that only people intended to see that data or communication can do so.

Example

Cryptography is an example of technology that can provide privacy.

Integrity

Integrity is knowing that the data sent has not been altered along the way.

Example

Cryptography, using digital signatures, is an example of technology that can provide integrity.

Putting the Concepts Together

Consider the case of a remote workstation connecting to a World Wide Web service on a host. First, the workstation is identified using authentication; it is who it claims to be. Second, access control is used to determine if the workstation can use the service it requested (the World Wide Web service).

Because the data being sent over the connection is encrypted, the data is kept private. You also can be certain of the data's integrity because it has been signed by the workstation.

Cryptography

Cryptography is a mechanism of coding, or disguising, data into an unreadable format so that only the people who are allowed to read or access that data can do so. In that way, the privacy of the data and of the individuals is protected.

Cryptography involves a mathematical *algorithm* and one or more secret values, known as *keys*. The algorithms can be public and well known; the key is the secret part of cryptography. To encrypt something, you start with a particular mathematical algorithm and then you "plug" a key into that algorithm.

There are various kinds of encryption algorithms. Some of the more well-known ones are listed below.

- The Digital Encryption Standard (DES) has been endorsed by the U. S. National Institute of Standards and Technology since 1975. DES is subject to United States export control. DES is a shared-key system.
- RSA (named for its creators' initials) is a public-key system and is patented technology in the United States.
- Diffie-Hellman is a public-key system that provides a shared, secret key.

Key Technology

This section discusses three types of key technology used in cryptography: shared-key, public-key, and Diffie-Hellman key technology.

Shared-Key Technology

Shared-key technology (also called *symmetric* key technology or secret-key technology) requires one key, which must be kept secret among its users.

Figure 3-1 illustrates the use of secret-key technology to keep data confidential between two users. In the figure, plain text (also called clear text) in a file is *encrypted* by a user with a secret key to create unreadable text, known as *ciphertext*; the ciphertext is then transmitted to the intended recipient, for example, by electronic mail; the recipient then *decrypts* the cipher text using the same secret key to re-create the original plain text.

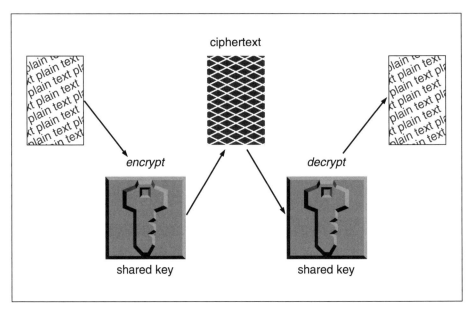

Figure 3-1   Shared-Key Technology

Shared-key technology allows for privacy because only the people who have the secret key can encrypt or decrypt the data. In shared-key technology, you need to have a mechanism to distribute the shared key in a protected way to the parties involved. Shared-key technology does not allow you to authenticate the source of the encrypted data, because anyone with the shared key could be the source of the communication.

Public-Key Technology

Public-key technology (also called *asymmetric* key technology) requires two asymmetric keys: one public key (that is deliberately made public) and one corresponding private key (that is kept absolutely private) per user.

The two keys are mathematically related so that data encrypted with a public key can only be decrypted with the corresponding private key; data encrypted with a private key can only be decrypted with the corresponding public key. The mathematics are such that even knowing a public key of a key pair, a person would not be able to figure out the corresponding private key.

Figure 3-2 illustrates the use of public-key technology to keep data confidential between two users. User #2 has a public/private key pair unique to him. He has given his public key to several people. In the figure, User #1 encrypts plain text in a file with User #2's *public key*; User #1 sends User #2 the encrypted message by electronic mail; User #2 then decrypts the message using his *private key*. User #2 is the only person who can decrypt the message that was encrypted with his public key.

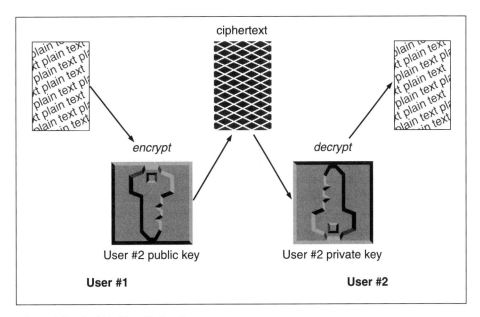

Figure 3-2   Public-Key Technology

Diffie-Hellman Key Technology

Diffie-Hellman, a type of public-key technology, includes the concept of a third key, the "shared, secret key." Figure 3-3 shows the use of this technology to encrypt data.

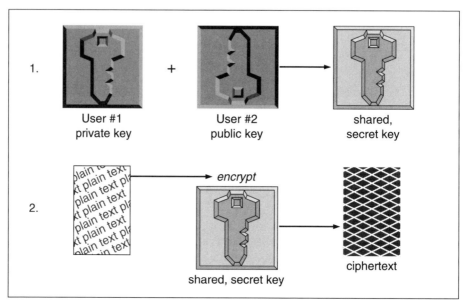

Figure 3-3   Using Diffie-Hellman Key Technology to Encrypt

User #1 starts with his private key and, using a Diffie-Hellman mathematical formula, combines it with User #2's public key; the result is a shared, secret key. User #1 then encrypts his message, using an algorithm (for example, DES) and the shared, secret key, and sends it to User #2.

At the receiving end, the process is reversed. User #2 starts with his private key and, using a Diffie-Hellman mathematical formula, combines it with User #1's public key; this computation results in the *identical* shared, secret key that User #1 used. User #2 can then decrypt the message by using the same algorithm and the same shared, secret key used by User #1.

Other public-key technologies, such as RSA, can also be used to create *digital signatures* to prove the identify of the sender. A mathematical algorithm is used to generate a *hash digest* of the data; the digest is then encrypted with the sender's private key. The result is called the digital signature of the document. The receiver also calculates the hash digest of the data, decrypts the encrypted hash digest by using the sender's public key, and compares these numbers for proof of authentication. The receiver thus completes the verification.

Thus, public-key technology can provide privacy and authentication of data. However, the mathematical operations involved in public-key operations make it slower than the simpler symmetric key technology. Because of this, practical cryptographic systems use some combination of both shared- and public-key technology.

Public-Key Certificates

A digital *certificate* can be thought of as a kind of credential. It makes a connection between a particular user and that particular user's public key. A certificate contains, and binds, your unique identity (your *name*) to your public key in a trustworthy manner. A certificate is also a way to make your public key available to others so they can use it for cryptographic operations.

Figure 3-4 shows the contents of a signed certificate.

Figure 3-4   Certificate Contents

Before a certificate can be used, it must be validated. You must be able to prove that the owner's name and the owner's public key are indeed bound together. There are several methods of doing this, as described in the next sections.

Signed Certificates

A *certificate authority* (CA) is a trusted person or institution that *signs* certificates. The CA obtains proper identification from a user before issuing that user a certificate and thus can vouch for the identity of the user for whom the CA is signing a certificate. The public key for which the CA generates a certificate must be the public component of a keypair. This keypair may have been generated by the user or may have been generated by the CA on behalf of the user.

The CA's own public key must be trustworthy. The CA must make known its public key or provide a certificate from a higher-level CA who vouches for the CA's identity and public key.

Self-Signed Certificates

Sometimes a CA does not exist to sign certificates. In this case, the certificate itself may be unsigned and the verification performed by manually transferring the certificate's signature between the two parties.

Unsigned Diffie-Hellman (UDH) certificates are an example of this kind of certificate verification; they can be generated on demand by a user in a system with SunScreen™ SKIP installed. They are verified by manually transferring the signature, which in this case is the same value as the owner's SKIP identity.

Simple Key-Management for Internet Protocols (SKIP)

SunScreen SKIP provides a secure communication channel between two hosts. The SKIP encryption technology provides a system with SKIP installed with the ability to encrypt all traffic to any SKIP-enabled product, including SunScreen EFS and SunScreen SPF-200.

SunScreen SKIP can be used on internal networks and over the Internet, wherever authentication and privacy of data are critical.

SunScreen SKIP uses the principles of Diffie-Hellman keys to generate shared, secret keys that only the sender and the receiver can use. SunScreen SKIP can use certificates signed by the Sun Microsystems Certificate Authority (SunCA) or can use self-signed (unsigned) Diffie-Hellman certificates.

How the SunScreen Firewalls Work   4 ≡

As discussed previously, a firewall sits between two or more networks and examines data that comes to it. It allows the data to pass through it or stops the data, according to the rules you have set up.

This chapter provides an introduction to the two SunSoft™ firewalls: the SunScreen EFS (Release 2.0) and the SunScreen SPF-200 (Release 1.0).

Overview and Diagrams

Both SunScreen EFS and SunScreen SPF-200 have two components: the *Screen* and the *Administration Station*. The Screen contains the rules and filters all packet traffic; the Administration Station configures and administers the Screen.

For the SPF-200, the two components must be on physically separate machines. For the EFS, the two components may or may not be on the same physical machine, depending on how you want to configure your network.

The EFS and SPF-200 Screens can be remotely administered over a network because the administrative traffic is secure (encrypted). Remote administration allows you to monitor and control your network security system from a central location. It saves time and money because people do not have to travel to the physical location of their Screens.

Figure 4-1 and Figure 4-2 show examples of basic network configurations with the EFS and the SPF-200, respectively.

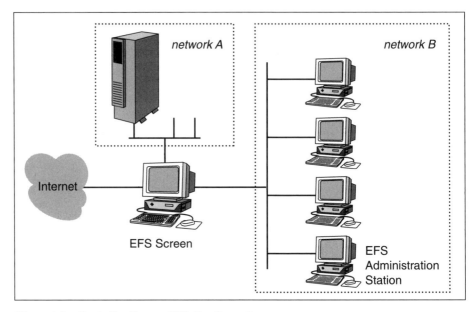

Figure 4-1   Basic SunScreen EFS Configuration

Because SunScreen EFS can be used to route packets, each of the networks attached to it must be a separate network or subnetwork, as shown in Figure 4-1. Network A and network B have different network addresses. So, when adding an EFS system to an existing network, you either (1) create a new network or (2) divide the existing network into *subnets*.

Subnetting gives you flexibility in how you use your network. Subnetting is a way of increasing the number of networks that you have, while decreasing the number of hosts per network.

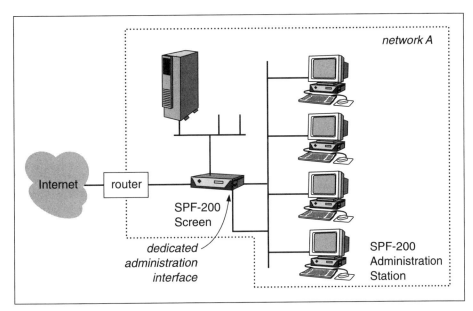

Figure 4-2   Basic SunScreen SPF-200 Configuration

In contrast to the SunScreen EFS, the SPF-200 is designed to divide *one* network into different pieces. The Screen can protect many networks, but it cannot route packets; therefore, its filtering interfaces must all be dividing a single network (network A in Figure 4-2). It does not divide the network into subnets; it is still one network as far as IP is concerned. One benefit from this approach is that when the SPF-200 is added to an existing network, the hosts on this network do not need to have new IP addresses assigned to them because they are still on the same network. Also, the SPF-200 must have one interface dedicated *solely* to administration, as shown in Figure 4-2.

Both the EFS and the SPF-200 products support the SKIP protocol. Each product gets its SKIP functionality by using the SKIP packages, which are bundled with the product. The strength of the encryption supported depends on the SKIP code included with the product.

How the Screen Checks Packet Traffic

When a packet arrives from the network, it enters the SunScreen EFS or SPF-200 Screen through a network interface, such as qe0. After that, it goes through a series of modules where various checks are performed.

Figure 4-3 shows how packets move through the Screen. A packet can be denied and dropped at various locations as it is checked by the Screen. No packet is forwarded unless it is expressly permitted by a rule.

Packet logging and SNMP alerts can be turned on for packets that are passed or dropped.

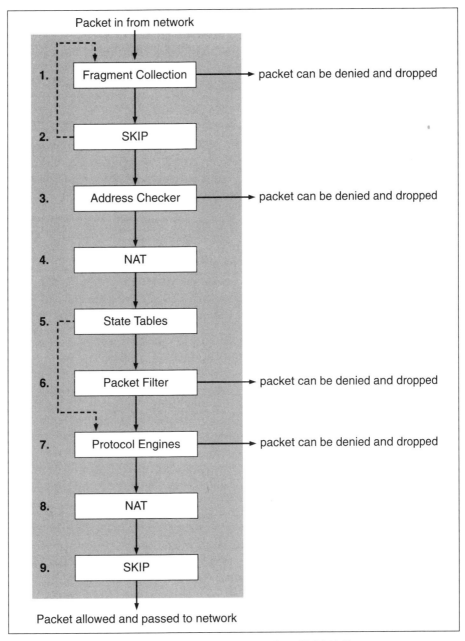

Figure 4-3   Packet Flow through a SunScreen EFS or SPF-200 Screen

The description of the packet flow shown in Figure 4-3 is as follows:

1. A packet arrives at the Screen from the network and enters the Screen through a network interface. Because packet fragmentation may occur over TCP/IP networks, the first thing the Screen does is collect all the packet fragments. If all the packet fragments cannot be collected, the packet is denied and dropped.

2. The packet passes through the SKIP module. If the packet is not encrypted, the packet passes to the address checker. However, if decryption is required, the packet is decrypted in the SKIP module and sent back through the packet assembly module. If the packet fragments do not assemble correctly, the packet is denied and dropped.

3. The address checker verifies the validity of the source and destination addresses by looking in the configuration files. If the packet contains an invalid source or destination address, it is denied and dropped. Otherwise, it passes to the NAT module.

4. In the NAT module, public addresses are translated to private addresses if necessary. The packet then passes to the state tables.

5. State tables keep certain information about *connections*. Connections can be as complicated as a TCP connection, or they can be as simple as a UDP request and response.

   The information kept includes items such as time-out information, the end points of the connection (addresses, ports), and other related connections for a session. For example, if a name service request is made, a state table entry is created that contains the end points of the connection (UDP request and response); when the response is received, it can be matched against the entry in the state table and safely passed through the Screen.

   All incoming packets are initially checked against existing state table entries. If state does not exist for a packet, the packet passes to the packet filter module. If state information exists for the packet, the packet passes directly to the appropriate protocol engine, rather than to the packet filter module; this design helps to improve performance.

6. In the packet filter (also referred to as the *PFL* engine, for packet filtering language), the packet is checked against the rules in your active configuration. If the packet matches a rule to allow the traffic, the rule tells

the Screen which protocol engine to pass the packet to. If the packet matches a rule to deny that traffic, the packet is denied and dropped. If the packet does not match a rule, it is denied and dropped.

7. The protocol engines have information about specific protocols, for example, FTP, RPC, and NFS. They know how each protocol manages connections. The protocol engines monitor data going over existing connections, manage the state table entries, and allow or disallow an operation based on user-specified requests. For example, if a user requests an NFS-write operation, the NFS read-only protocol engine would deny the request because that operation is not allowed. A protocol engine may also add entries in the state table. For example, the FTP protocol engine monitors traffic over the ftp connection, watching for PORT commands; when it sees a PORT command, it extracts the data connection information from the command, and adds a new state table entry to the Screen to allow that data connection.

   The protocol engines also validate the data received over a connection. If there is a problem with the data, for example, if a port number in the ftp PORT command is too small, the packet is denied and dropped by the protocol engine. If a packet is not dropped by the protocol engine, it passes to the NAT module.

8. In the NAT module, private addresses are translated to public addresses, if necessary. The packet then passes to the SKIP module.

9. In the SKIP module, the packet is encrypted if required. The packet then passes from the Screen out to the network.

All firewall systems have some performance degradation. As a firewall is busy checking or rerouting data packets, the packets do not flow through the system as efficiently as they would if the system were not in place. You can take steps, such as optimizing your rules, to help performance. This topic is discussed in Chapter 6, "Translating Your Security Policy to Your SunScreen Firewalls."

The SunScreen EFS Firewall

SunScreen EFS is a software product designed to be added to an existing Solaris system that may already be acting as a router. SunScreen EFS makes use of the Solaris IP protocol stack.

SunScreen EFS can be administered either locally (one system functions as both the Screen and the Administration Station) or remotely (one system functions as the Screen, another system functions as the Administration Station) from a Solaris system running SKIP. Administration can be done using a command-line interface or through a Java™-based graphical user interface (GUI).

Depending upon how a site decides to implement SunScreen EFS, the number of Screens and Administration Stations will vary. Only one Administration Station is needed to manage multiple Screens, although more can be used for redundancy and ease of access.

SunScreen EFS 2.0 is supported in the Solaris 2.5.1 and 2.6 operating environments.

The SunScreen SPF-200 Firewall

SunScreen SPF-200[1] consists of two software components—a Screen and an Administration Station—that must reside on two physically separate machines. The SPF-200 Screen host is a headless (that is, no monitor, no keyboard) hardware host. Unlike the EFS, the SPF-200 does not use the Solaris IP protocol stack; it has an IP address, but it is designed so that it only allows communication with that address by means of SKIP and only with its known Administration Stations. It is a *stealthy* machine (that is, it cannot be detected or "seen" by someone looking for machine IP addresses) and cannot be used as a router.

The SunScreen SPF-200 Screen has predefined software and is a dedicated firewall. The first thing that happens when the Screen is installed is that the hard drive is reformatted and *only* the SPF-200 software from the product CD is installed. You cannot add other packages or software to the Screen itself. The only communication from the Administration Station to the Screen uses SKIP encryption, and it occurs only through the software tools that are provided (such as the commands `sas_main`, `sas_registry`, and `ss_client`).

The SunScreen SPF-200 Screen is based on the Solaris 2.5.1 operating environment. The SunScreen SPF-200 Administration Station is supported on the Solaris 2.4, 2.5, and 2.5.1 operating environments.

---

1. SunScreen SPF-100, the precursor to the SunScreen SPF-200, works in a similar manner, although it is not covered by this book. The SPF-100 product is a hardware and software combination solution. The SunScreen SPF-200 can be installed on top of the SPF-100 or on a dedicated machine.

Explanation of Some Differences

The main differences between the SunScreen EFS and the SPF-200 firewalls are in their operating environment, how they fit into a network, and how they check rules.

Operating Environment and Networks

SunScreen EFS has the full Solaris operating environment. SunScreen EFS can be used as a router. Additional Solaris packages can be installed on an EFS system.

For the SPF-200, the Solaris operating environment has been "hardened," or "stripped down," to provide a minimum of service (for example, the Console window has been removed); you must administer it from another machine. The SPF-200 has no IP address on interfaces other than on its dedicated administration interface. Hence, the SPF-200 cannot be used as a router; however, this also means that it can't be detected with *snooping*[1]. The SPF-200 requires a dedicated port for administration.

The SPF-200 is designed to divide a single network without requiring any special effort with network addresses. The EFS is usually used with subnetworks, and you may need to do some readdressing to place an EFS in an existing network.

SunScreen SPF supports Ethernet interfaces only. SunScreen EFS supports additional connections, such as ATM and FDDI.

Rules

In SunScreen EFS 2.0, rules are ordered, that is, they are numbered and take effect according to the order you have chosen. When a packet is checked against the rules, it is checked for a match against rule #1 first, then rule #2, then rule #3, and so on.

In SunScreen SPF-200 1.0, rules follow an encrypt-pass-fail scenario. When a packet is checked against the rules, an encryption rule takes precedence over pass or fail rules; a pass rule takes precedence over a fail rule.

---

1. snoop is a program that captures packets from the network and displays their contents.

Managing SunScreen Firewalls 5 ≡

This chapter discusses administration of your SunScreen firewalls.[1]

What Does Administration Include?

As a system or network administrator for the SunScreen EFS or SPF-200 products, you should be concerned with these general activities:

- Being involved with your organization's security policy
- Monitoring the SunScreen EFS and SPF-200 firewalls
- Translating the security policy into rules; this activity is discussed in Chapter 6, "Translating Your Security Policy to Your SunScreen Firewalls"
- Understanding what it means to allow access to different services; understanding the risks of allowing or disallowing each service
- Determining the best location for firewalls (being involved with network topology, subnetting, and other network issues)
- Developing a process for backup of information on firewalls
- Determining what to do in the event of a failure of a firewall
- Securing any systems being used as SunScreen Administration Stations. For example, you might want to limit the number of users with access to an Administration Station and limit the network services allowed to run on that machine. You want to make sure that no one can break into an Administration Station and pretend to be an administrator of the firewall.

---

1. The SunScreen product documentation contains complete details on administration.

- Determining how you are going to manage SunScreen SKIP. For example, how will keys be generated? How will you, as the administrator, get the users' certificates securely?

Interacting with the Screen

For administration, EFS 2.0 uses a Java GUI and the command line. Any actions taken in the GUI can also be issued as commands on the command line. This scenario is shown in Figure 5-1.

The SPF-200 uses an X-based GUI for the `sas_main` (rules) program and the `sas_registry` (SKIP information) program, and the command line for the `ss_client` command. Any actions taken in the GUI can also be issued as commands on the command line. This scenario is shown in Figure 5-2.

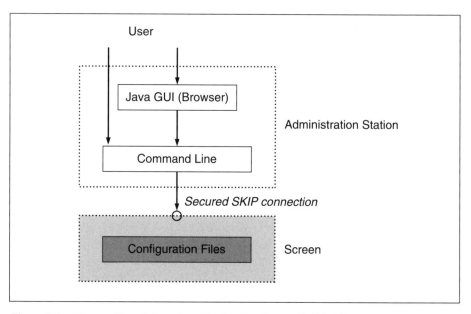

Figure 5-1   How a User Interacts with the SunScreen EFS 2.0 Screen

On an EFS 2.0 system, you can use either the Java GUI interface in a browser, or you can use the command line to communicate with the Screen. The GUI actually works by calling the appropriate commands from the command line.

On an EFS Screen, the ports can be shared between administration and packet filtering. On an SPF-200 Screen, the ports are dedicated for specific services; there must be a dedicated port for SPF-200 administration.

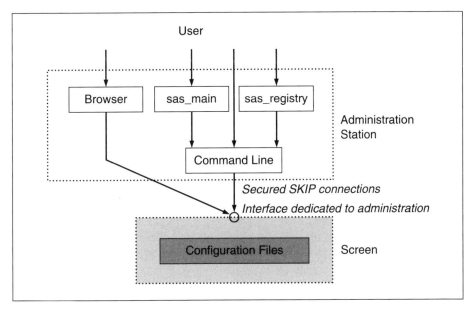

Figure 5-2   How a User Interacts with the SunScreen SPF-200 Screen

Using the SunScreen EFS and SPF-200 Firewalls Together

You can use the SunScreen EFS and SPF-200 products on the same network. From one Solaris machine, you can administer multiple SPF-200 machines or multiple EFS machines.

To administer multiple SunScreen EFS and SPF-200 Screens from a single Solaris Administration Station, you must have installed the administration packages from both the EFS and the SPF-200 software; you should also be using the HotJava™ browser. Note that the "look and feel" of the EFS and SPF-200 administration interfaces is different.

An Example Use

Figure 5-3 shows an example use of the SunScreen EFS and SPF-200 products together. The figure shows an organization's main site (headquarters), a remote site, and an employee somewhere with a laptop computer.

At headquarters, the SPF-200 Screen isolates the DMZ with the World Wide Web server and protects all the intranets. The EFS Screens further divide the network and are routers to the intranets at headquarters; they are used for packet screening. You can run additional software on the EFS Screens as well; however, make sure that having the additional software doesn't pose a security threat for the firewall itself because they are on the same machine.

The EFS/SPF-200 Administration Station #1 administers both EFS Screens and the SPF-200 Screen. To do this, you added a rule to EFS Screen #1 to allow SKIP traffic to pass between EFS Administration Station #1 and EFS Screen #2 and the SPF-200 Screen. Adding this rule allows you to administer multiple Screens from one location.

A virtual private network (VPN) has been set up between the two SunScreen SPF-200s. Traffic between these two hosts is through an encrypted tunnel, ensuring privacy of data.

The laptop user can be anywhere; he might be in a hotel room, making a connection to headquarters through an ISP account, for example. He has SunScreen SKIP on his laptop and makes an encrypted connection to the SPF-200 at headquarters. The SPF-200 authenticates him and allows him to connect to the machine he wants, for example, he may want to read his email or access a server with internal marketing data on it. Traffic between the two hosts is encrypted, ensuring privacy of data.

With this network setup, you (1) allow unencrypted traffic to your DMZ network only, that is, people outside your organization can access the DMZ and the web server, but the SPF-200 prevents them from getting to any other Intranet; (2) control access of your users to Internet sites; and (3) provide encrypted traffic between two firewalls (the two SunScreen SPF-200s) using a VPN, and encrypted traffic between the laptop user and the SunScreen SPF-200 at headquarters. The VPN protects data where it's most vulnerable to attack and compromise.

You control traffic between networks (source and destination IP addresses), then control which systems communicate with each other (source and destination IP addresses), what services they use (specified in rules), and then, optionally, whether to use cryptography (SKIP identities).

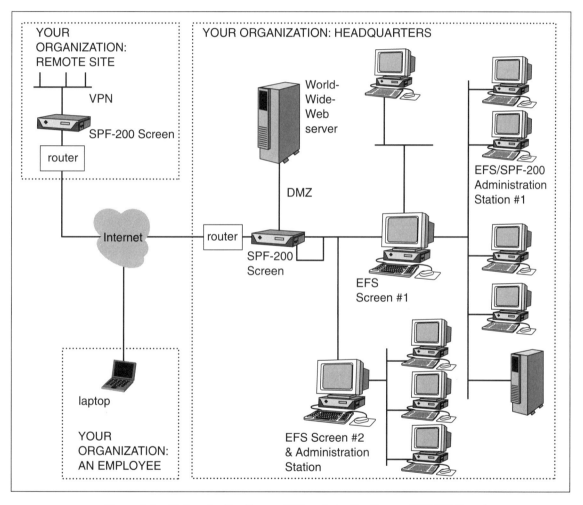

Figure 5-3   Using the SunScreen EFS and the SunScreen SPF-200 Together

Backward Compatibility

SunScreen EFS and the SPF-200 can be used on the same network. They both use SKIP to communicate, and you can build VPNs between them. Both products also support SKIP Version 1, which can be used to communicate with the older SunScreen SPF-100 systems.

Administration is not completely backward-compatible with previous versions of the products. As an example, SunScreen EFS 2.0 is the only version of the products with a Java-based GUI. You can't use the SunScreen EFS 2.0 GUI to edit configurations on an SPF-200 system, and vice versa.

EFS Administration

On the EFS Screen, local administration acquires a new meaning because the administrative software can run on the same host as the Screen software. This is possible because the EFS Screen has a monitor and a keyboard (unlike the SPF-200 Screen). There is no need for a dedicated administrative port on an EFS Screen.

Thus, for an EFS Screen, local administration means administrative tasks are performed on the same host that runs the Screen software, and remote administration means administrative tasks are performed on any other host that may be running the administrative software and accessing the Screen over a network. The remote administration station can be on the local network or on a more distant network; it makes no difference.

Encryption still needs to be configured on an EFS Screen, but it is not necessary to add rules to enable packets to pass through special ports. Administrative security is controlled by means of certificates, the Administrative Access Control entries, and passwords, rather than by configuring packet screen rules.

For SunScreen EFS 2.0, you can use the GUI or the command line to administer Screens. If you use the GUI, you administer Screens in a Screen-by-Screen fashion. You can bring up multiple browsers at a time to administer different Screens; however, you cannot control multiple Screens (that is, define and load rules to many Screens with a single operation) at the same time from a single Administration Station.

There are ways you can make the EFS Screen itself more secure. You can disable or remove unneeded services from the Solaris operating environment for the SunScreen EFS Screen (these services have already been removed from the operating environment shipped with the SPF-200). This can be done by disabling network services (such as `fingerd`) in the `/etc/inetd.conf` directory, deleting binaries (such as `ftpd`), and editing or deleting scripts in the `/etc/init.d` directory that start unneeded services. For additional security, you could make sure that your rules only allow administration to the EFS Screen and that no other services are allowed; log the administration traffic and check the logs regularly.

High Availability

SunScreen EFS 2.0 includes the capability to set up and administer high availability. High availability includes a redundant Screen, that is, a Screen that is passively watching data while the active Screen is doing the actual packet filtering. The Screens are identically configured, so that in the event the active Screen ceases to function, the redundant Screen detects the failure and automatically takes over the routing and filtering of network traffic.

Proxies

SunScreen EFS 2.0 also includes a limited capability to set up a proxy for FTP, TELNET, HTTP, and SMTP. These proxies are separate user-level applications; their main purpose is to provide some content filtering and user authentication. You can allow or deny sessions based on the source and destination addresses. The proxies reside on the Screen at their standard port numbers.

Table 5-1 briefly describes the proxies.

Table 5-1   SunScreen EFS 2.0 Proxies

Proxy	Description
FTP	Provides control of File Transfer Protocol (FTP) commands based on user authentication
TELNET	Provides a "virtual" terminal based on user authentication
HTTP	Provides World Wide Web content filtering, for example, the ability to filter Java applets
SMTP	Provides mail filtering, for example, the ability to filter mail from unsolicited (spam) domains

SPF-200 Administration

For the SPF-200, the Screen and the Administration software must be on two separate machines. The administration software requires a dedicated port on the Screen.

The SPF-200 Screen's filtering interfaces must all subdivide one network. (You specify this single network either on the HTML GUI Interfaces Page or by using the ss_network command on the command line.) The administration interface can be on a different network from the packet filtering interfaces.

For remote administration, you must add authorized administration users. Then, if there are any firewalls between the Administration Station and the Screen being administered, you must add rules on those intermediate firewalls to allow SKIP traffic to pass between the Administration Station and the firewall being administered.

Once you add the administrator's certificate to the Screen's certificate database and add the remote workstation to the access control list (ACL), you can add a new security system administrator's user ID and password to the HTML Manager's access list. Finally, define the appropriate ACL entry for the Screen on the remote Administration Station.

Some Administration Scenarios

This section describes some of the commonly performed administrative tasks.

Adding Another Remote Administration Station

When might you want additional remote Administration Stations? For example, your organization might have multiple network operations centers, some in different states or countries, and you might want to be able to administer Screens from different locations.

Figure 5-4 illustrates the use of a SunScreen EFS with several Administration Stations, one of them at a remote site. Any of these Administration Stations can administer the EFS Screen.

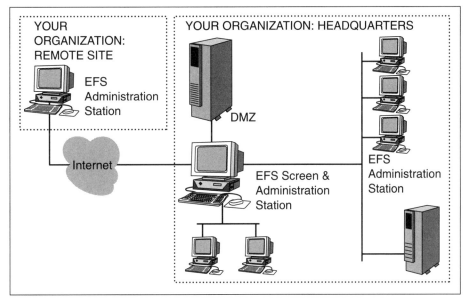

Figure 5-4   Using Multiple Administration Stations

Remote administration uses encryption to protect access and to limit management of a Screen to an authorized Administration Station.

Using Another Machine as an Administration Station

To change which machine you use as the Administration Station, add the new machine to be used as the Administration Station; when the new Administration Station is functioning, use it to remove old Administration Station access.

Copying a Configuration

It is possible to add another Screen to do everything an existing Screen does. This involves copying a configuration.

In addition to copying the configuration (which includes the rules), you also must make sure that you have entered all the addresses you need.

Creating Address Lists

SunScreen products use IP addresses to define the network elements that make up configurations. These addresses are then used in defining the network interfaces and as the source and destination addresses for rules. The IP address can define a single computer, a whole network, or a subnetwork.

IP addresses (computer and network) can be grouped to form an *address list*. You can define address lists that specifically include or exclude certain IP addresses and ranges of addresses.

Understanding Packet Traffic on the Network Protocol Stack

It's important to remember one of the distinctions between the SunScreen SPF-200 Screen and SunScreen EFS Screen.

On a SunScreen SPF-200 Screen, for each filtering interface, there is no IP stack, hence no IP address. The SunScreen SPF-200 looks at every packet on the network, including the non-IP traffic. In general, this non-IP traffic is not passed.

On a SunScreen EFS Screen, for each filtering interface, the EFS module is layered between the network interface and the IP stack. It will see (and thus be able to filter) only packets that are being sent on the IP stack. The SunScreen EFS can act as a router.

The hierarchy associated with IP traffic, as shown in Figure 5-5, has implications for SunScreen rules. IP rules override TCP or UDP rules. In EFS 2.0, which has ordered rules, you should place any TCP or UDP rule before an IP rule if you want it to be considered first. As a general guideline, you should place the more specific rules first.

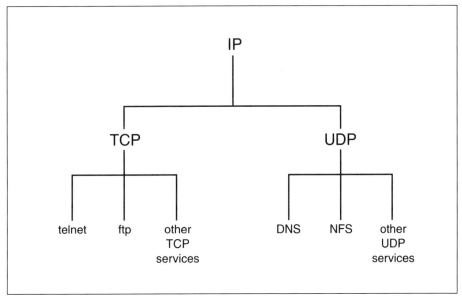

Figure 5-5 IP Traffic Hierarchy

After a packet is allowed, the SPF-200 passes the packet to a specific interface that you have indicated in your rules; the EFS passes the packet to IP. In the case of the EFS, IP then passes the packet according to its (IP's) rules. IP rules may or may not be consistent with your security policy. As an example, consider broadcast packets. Under IP rules, broadcast packets are delivered to all machines with IP addresses, including the EFS Screen. Broadcast packets cannot be delivered to an SPF-200 Screen because it doesn't have an IP address on its filtering interfaces.

Communicating Securely with SKIP

SunScreen SKIP (Simple Key-Management for Internet Protocols) is the technology used by the SunScreen products to communicate securely. When you use SunScreen SKIP technology, you:

- Encrypt and decrypt data
- Provide authentication

SunScreen SKIP can be installed on an end-system host, such as a laptop, a PC, a workstation, and so on; SunScreen SKIP is also an embedded part of the SunScreen EFS and SunScreen SPF-200 products. The communication between a SunScreen Administration Station and a Screen is encrypted by means of SKIP technology.

How SKIP Works

SKIP works according to the principles of Diffie-Hellman key technology, as illustrated in Figure 5-6.

In Figure 5-6, the host system with SunScreen EFS, SunScreen SPF-200, or end-system SKIP installed starts by using SKIP's random number generator to generate its private key. The private key is then used in two subsequent, separate operations: (1) creating the public key and certificate and (2) creating the shared, secret key.

In the first operation, the private key is run through a Diffie-Hellman mathematical formula to produce the host's public key; the public key is then made a part of (included in) the host's certificate. The certificate is the way to distribute a public key in a verifiable manner. When a host needs another host's public key, it requests the other host's certificate either by using Certificate Discovery Protocol (CDP)[1] over a network or by retrieving the certificate from its database where the certificate was installed directly by the user.

In the second operation, the private key is combined with the receiver's public key (extracted from the receiver's certificate) and run through a Diffie-Hellman mathematical formula to create the shared, secret key. The shared, secret key is then plugged into the specified encryption algorithm (such as DES) and used to encrypt a *traffic key*. The traffic key has been generated with a random number generator. The traffic key is used to encrypt the data. Both the encrypted traffic key and the encrypted data are sent to the remote system.

When the host with SKIP enabled receives the encrypted traffic key and data, a Diffie-Hellman mathematical formula combines the receiver's private key with the sender's public key to create the shared, secret key. The results of this computation create the identical shared, secret key calculated by the sender. SKIP then decrypts the traffic key by using the shared, secret key and, finally, decrypts the message by using the traffic key.

---

1. CDP is a request-and-response protocol used in transferring certificates between two parties.

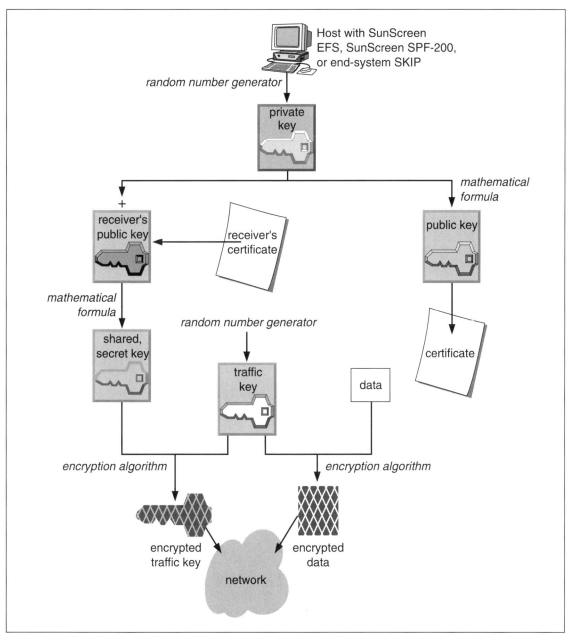

Figure 5-6   Illustration of SKIP Using Diffie-Hellman Key Technology

SKIP uses either:

- Unsigned Diffie-Hellman (UDH), also called self-signed, keys and certificates. The user generates these keys. (Note that UDH does not work with the SunScreen SPF-100.)
- Signed SunCA key pair and certificate. These are obtained on diskette from Sun Microsystems, Inc., and are installed by the user.

The decision whether to use signed or self-signed certificates depends on your security policy and the type of host with which you want to exchange encrypted data. For example, self-signed certificates might be used when there is no need for a trusted third party to sign a certificate, as in the case of encrypting communications between different sites of the same organization. Signed certificates, on the other hand, might be used if outside parties are involved or if there is a need for user authentication.

In order to have a successful encrypted connection between two SKIP hosts, the keys on the two machines must be the same length, and the hosts must be able to exchange their public certificates (by using a diskette or CDP), extract each other's public key out of the public certificate, and calculate the shared, secret key. The results of this calculation must be identical on each side.

There are times when it is useful to allow a system to have more than one pair of public-private keys. For example, different key sizes may be required when communicating with subsidiaries in other countries because of U.S. or local regulations. SunScreen SKIP allows a system to have multiple local keys.

Example

The SPF-200 Screen can have multiple types of local identities, using its 1024-bit SunCA certificates when communicating with PCs that use SunCA certificates, using its 512-bit SunCA global certificate with PCs that use SunCA global certificates, and so forth.

SKIP in SunScreen Firewalls and SKIP on an End System

SunScreen SKIP end-system nodes use access control lists (ACLs) to determine whether remote hosts or networks are authorized to communicate with your computer. Each entry in an ACL identifies a specific host (by name or by IP address) or a network (by network number and a subnet mask).

Screens control access by means of rules. If you want to pass SKIP traffic through Screens, you have to write a rule to let it pass.

ACLs and rules are really two names for the same thing. The difference is that Screens allow more specific control than end-system SKIP nodes (for example, access control by service rather than by IP address).

Monitoring

There are various ways to monitor your firewall implementation. This section describes using logs, using SNMP alerts, and checking firewall status.

Using Logs

A log is a record of computer or network activities. Logs typically include items of data such as date, time, computer identification, and what occurred.

Logs can be divided into two general categories: system logs and packet logs. System logs usually occur at the operating system level; an example of a system log is the `lastlog` file the Solaris operating environment generates. Packet logs record information about packet traffic; packet logs can be generated by firewalls that have the capability to examine traffic at the packet level.

Why Logs Are Useful

Logs are a useful tool to monitor computer and network activities. You can check logs for usual activity and for unusual activity. For example, perhaps someone is transferring many files with ftp from a particular server; this might be okay, but it might not be okay if the transfer occurred from a server you didn't expect someone to be accessing. You can use logs to keep track of how your firewall is being used. Logs are also useful for statistical purposes: they can be useful for billing or for auditing connections.

Some suggested items to look for in logs include:

- Attacks to servers, file servers, and authentication machines; an attempted telnet to a web server
- Anything that looks odd on an important server
- Something that happens over and over. This should be investigated. It might or might not be a legitimate occurrence

- Packets that get dropped. You'll need to determine whether or not the person was trying to do something destructive

How To Use SunScreen Logs

The SunScreen EFS and SPF-200 firewalls provide packet logging capability. Packet logging can occur on a packet-by-packet basis (each packet is examined) or on a *session* basis (groups of packets are examined).

You specify whether you want your SunScreen firewall to do logging when you write a rule. Whatever you have in your rules controls what data is logged.

Some of the items you might consider logging are:

- Packets that are dropped
- Packets that are passed
- Session data

If you are logging packets that are dropped, as you examine the log files, you should ask this question: why did a particular packet get dropped? There are various reasons why a packet could be dropped. It is possible that you actually wanted to allow the packet to pass but you incorrectly translated your policy to a rule that caused the packet to be dropped. In this case, you would fix the incorrect rule so that the packet would be allowed to pass.

The other possibility if a packet is dropped happens when the traffic was intentionally not allowed. In the case where you actually wanted to stop the packet from passing, there are two categories: the traffic could be harmless (for example, an external host sending an echo request by using the `ping` command to a single host on your internal network), or it could be harmful (for example, an external host sending an echo request to every host on your internal network). You must determine what is harmful for your organization.

There are performance considerations with logging every packet that passes. If you log all packets that are passed, you can accumulate large amounts of data in your log files. If you don't want the overhead of packet-by-packet logging, you can choose to collect reduced statistics on a group of packets, for example, all packets from an FTP session.

One of the dilemmas with logging is getting too much information. You want to be able to actually use the logs to help you understand events. If you find you are collecting too much information, ask yourself how you can log fewer events.

The SunScreen Log Browser

Under EFS 2.0, you can use the GUI Log Browser to view the log file; for the SPF-200, you use the command line to move the log from the Screen onto another machine to view the log file. One advantage of the GUI Log Browser over the command line is that the Log Browser shows data in "real time," that is, almost instantaneously as events are happening.

Figure 5-7 shows a portion of a sample log file in the EFS 2.0 Log Browser.

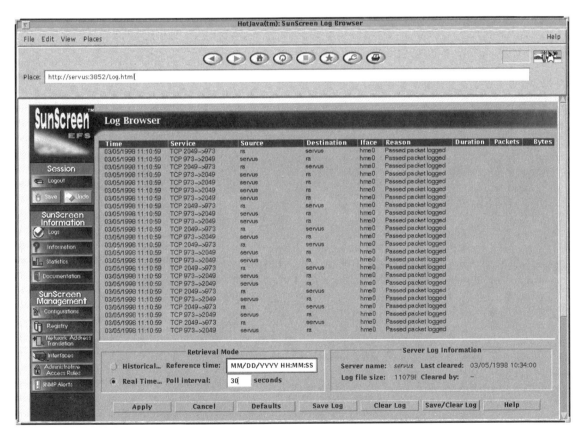

Figure 5-7   Sample Log File in the SunScreen EFS Log Browser

Similar information is given in ASCII format in the SPF-200 log file.

Storing SunScreen Logs

Log files can grow large. The Screen maintains the packet logs in a "circular" file of 100 one-megabyte files in its own storage; thus, the maximum size of the log file is 100 megabytes. When that number is reached, the Screen starts to overwrite the log file, overwriting the oldest file first.

It is helpful to occasionally check to see how large the log is. You could also copy or archive the log file to another machine that has more storage than the Screen.

Receiving SNMP Alerts

Simple Network Management Protocol (SNMP) is a standard for monitoring network devices. SNMP detects when certain, predefined events happen and "alerts" a designated network management station about the event.

The SunScreen firewalls include a management information base (MIB) and can generate SNMP alerts. You can specify whether you want an SNMP alert to be issued and, if so, which host should receive the alert. The network management station receiving the SNMP alerts cannot be the Administration Station; SNMP alerts are sent in the clear (unencrypted), and you can't mix encrypted and unencrypted traffic on a host running end-system SKIP.

The SNMP alert is part of the action associated with a rule.

Checking the Status of Your Firewalls

One way to check the status of your EFS Screens is by periodically using the ping command. Make sure you have allowed ping in your rules. If you don't expect to have ready access to an Administration Station all the time, you could write a script to have the command output sent to your pager.

For the SPF-200, you can use the ping command on the administration port only; the host sending the ping command must be set up to administer the SPF-200 (have the correct SKIP parameters, and so on).

Troubleshooting

This section contains some basic troubleshooting pointers to consider.

Routing

If you are going to use an EFS system, make sure that the Solaris host works correctly as a router first, before installing the EFS software. Check to see if your Solaris operating environment is configured correctly. If it's practical, try to pass traffic through the system first, before installing the EFS software.

If you are using an SPF-200 system and NAT or SKIP with tunneling, make sure that you've specified the default routes correctly; remember that the SPF-200 is not a router.

Services

Some services rely on other services to work correctly. For example, web services (such as HTTP) rely on routing and naming services. You should determine what, if any, routing protocols need to pass through the firewall. Your web server may need to reach a name server; so, for example, it may have to perform a DNS lookup. Problems with services can frequently be traced to routing or naming problems.

SKIP Connections

If a SKIP connection is not working properly, there are several things you can check.

- SKIP error messages are written to the SKIP log file, `/var/logs/skipd.log`.
- Check the expiration date on your certificates to make sure they have not expired.
- Each SKIP node must have an accurate notion of time. SKIP nodes can be located anywhere, but each node's notion of the time in GMT must be within one hour of the other node.

- Check the packet log file to see if a SKIP packet is being dropped. On the side where encryption is being done, if a packet is dropped before it is encrypted, the problem could be with the keys. On the decryption side, a dropped packet could indicate an access control problem or an encryption parameter error, such as different algorithms being used.

Logs

Regularly examine system logs and packet log files from your SunScreen EFS or SPF-200 firewall.

If you are logging packets that are dropped, you may be able to determine from the log file what, if anything, you might be missing in your rules or configuration that you need.

Programs to Generate Information

These commands generate information that can be helpful in determining the source of a problem: `snoop`, `ping`, and `traceroute`.

Translating Your Security Policy to Your SunScreen Firewalls 6 ☰

Once your policy is as complete as possible for your particular environment, you are ready to set up the rules for implementation of the SunScreen EFS or SPF-200 portion of your security policy. Both SunScreen EFS and SunScreen SPF-200 are rules-based stateful packet filters, so the set of rules, called a *configuration*, is the basis for managing your Internet and intranet access with them.

Since each packet sent through the SunScreen firewall will have to be compared against all rules until it finds an exact match, the goal in creating a configuration is to create the smallest number of rules necessary to implement your policy exactly. This strategy helps to avoid conflicting and redundant rules and overly large, unwieldy configurations.

Getting Organized

The first step in translating your security policy into a configuration for SunScreen EFS or SPF-200 is to assemble all the information you will need:

- A copy of your security policy

- A diagram of your network, called a Network Topology Map

- The IP addresses of all your network elements, including web servers, ftp servers, routers, and other individual machines that need special consideration, and the beginning addresses and ranges of your local and remote networks

Security Policy

Your security policy should provide answers with regard to security decisions such as:

- What Internet services to allow and deny
- Whether or not you are using network address translation, and where
- Who can access which portions of the network

Network Topology Map

The network topology and diagrams provide the visual representation of your network. They play an important part in managing your network in general and are particularly important in translating your security policy into a configuration.

Included in the diagrams are locations of servers, network management stations, and the locations of the Screens and Administration Stations. Also included are local and remote networks and individual machines such as routers, web and ftp servers, and proxy servers. Each individual machine should have its name, IP address, and location attached to it. Networks should show the network range. If you are using Network Address Translation (NAT), you should also indicate which addresses will be translated and to what address they will be translated.

Using Figure 6-1 as a reference, create the network map of the network to be protected by the SunScreen firewall. Later, this map is used to help position your SunScreen products, to define encrypted connections, to translate NAT addresses, and to create rules for single and group services.

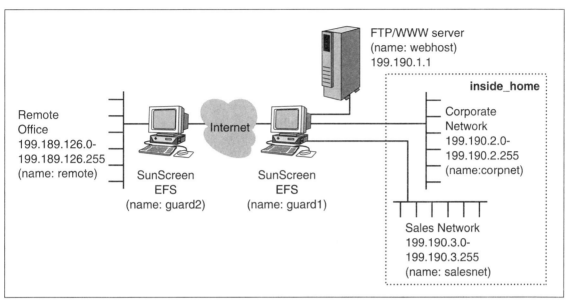

Figure 6-1 Sample Network Topology Map

IP Addresses

The next step in getting organized is to create a list of all the IP addresses that the SunScreen needs to know. SunScreen identifies network elements— network, subnetworks, and individual hosts—by IP address. Table 6-1 lists the types of addresses that can be defined in SunScreen products.

Table 6-1　Address Types

Address Type	Description	Example
Host Address	For individual elements, such as the router and individual computers. You need to know the IP address and the name of the element.	**name**: webhost **address**: 199.190.1.1
Address Range	For networks and subnetworks. You need to know the beginning address and the ending address of the network or subnetwork and a name for the network or subnetwork.	**name**: corpnet **Address range**: 199.190.2.1 - 199.190.2.255
Address List	Groups of host addresses, network addresses, and other Address Lists can be combined to form logical groups of addresses that can then be manipulated as a single element. Address lists are defined after all the host addresses and address ranges are defined. Lists may be inclusive or exclusive or a combination of both. Lists may not include themselves and may not include lists that contain themselves.	**name**: inside_home **elements**: corpnet, salesnet

In Figure 6-1, the following examples of different types of addresses can be seen:

- The FTP/WWW server is an example of a single host address (199.190.1.1).
- The corporate network, the sales network, and remote network are examples of address ranges. For example, the address range in the corporate network is defined as the group of addresses from 199.190.2.0 to 199.190.2.255, inclusive.
- Inside_home is an example of an address list, in this case defined as the address ranges for the corporate and sales networks.

Understanding Rules

Once you have finished gathering and creating the source material, the next step is to map the security policy to a rules configuration for your network. Up to this point, the focus has been on the concept of a rule as a whole. Now you are going to break down the rules into their elements.

SunScreen SPF-200 is designed so that you can define elements for a rule independently of the rule itself, thereby allowing elements to be reused in multiple rules as necessary, rather than having to redefine all the elements for each rule. SunScreen EFS lets you define the addresses and services separately; the remaining elements are defined when you create or modify the rule.

Basic Rule Elements

A rule tells the Screen what to do when it receives a packet of a certain type from a specific address or network going to a specific address or network governed by the configuration. All rules must have the following four elements to be a valid rule.

- Source Address ("From" Address)
- Destination Address ("To" Address)
- Rule Type
- Service (or group of services)

Source and Destination Addresses

The *Source Address*, also called the *From Address*, is the IP address initiating the connection. The *Destination Address*, also called the *To Address*, is the IP address of the recipient of the original packet. Addresses can be specified either as individual (host) addresses, address ranges, or address lists. Addresses can be either source or destination addresses. An address can be used in more than one rule or combined in more than one address list. The following table shows the address names of the individual components of the network shown in Figure 6-1.

Network Component	Address Name
FTP/WWW Server	webhost
Remote EFS Screen	guard2
Local EFS Screen	localhost

Network Component	Address Name
Corporate Network	corpnet
Sales Network	salesnet
Remote Network	remote

Address lists are helpful when you are grouping together individual hosts and subnetworks. For example, in Figure 6-1, you can group the corporate network and the sales network to form the address list **inside_home**. If you also include the local SunScreen and the FTP/WWW server, you can make another address list called **all_home**. The following table shows the address lists created from the network components listed in the previous table. Notice that the address list **all_home** contains the address list **inside_home**. This is acceptable so long as **inside_home** does not also contain **all_home**.

Address List Name	Addresses in List
inside_home	corpnet, salesnet
all_home	inside_home, webhost, localhost

For EFS 2.0, addresses are defined in the Registry page, under the Addresses tab. For SPF-200, addresses are defined in the Addresses window from the Configuration manager. Refer to the product documentation for complete instructions on how to set up addresses.

Rule Type

The Rule Type tells the Screen what to do with the packet that matches exactly with the service, source address, and destination address. The Rule Type is defined when the rule is created. Rules can be either *allow* or *deny*. An allow rule allows the packet to pass on to its destination. A deny rule tells the Screen to drop the packet. Both allow and deny rules have additional parameters that are specified at the time the rule is created. These additional parameters tell the Screen how to log packets that match the rule and what, if any, message to send back to the source of a packet that was dropped. Allow rules let you specify how the rule is logged and whether you want an SNMP alert sent when the rule is used. Deny rules also let you specify logging and SNMP alerts and have an additional field to let you specify what, if any, ICMP data is sent back to the sender. Table 6-2 summarizes the valid parameters for the rule types.

Table 6-2   Valid Parameters for Rule Types

Action	Parameters	Valid for Rule Type
log data	none summary detail session	Allow, Deny
SNMP data	SNMP none	Allow, Deny
ICMP data	none net unreachable host unreachable port unreachable net forbidden host forbidden	Deny

Service

Service specifies either an individual network service like telnet, gopher, or ftp, or a service group that combines multiple individual services into more meaningful sets, such as "allowed outbound services." This set is referred to as a *Service Group* and is extremely useful in reducing the number of rules to be written.

For example, suppose you have a host machine that is serving as an ftp, telnet, and HTTP server. Without using service groups, you need to write two rules for each service: one for the case when the packet is destined to the proper host machine, and one for the case when the packet is destined to anywhere else. You can either write six rules, two for each service, or you can group the three services together into one service group and create two rules for all three. The following table shows the rules without service groups. The table after that shows the same rules with a service group named Webservices. Both tables use the asterisk (*) to denote "anywhere," and the names are from Figure 6-1.

Without Service Groups:

Service	Source	Destination	Type
ftp	*	webhost	Allow, log none
ftp	*	inside_home	Deny, session log
telnet	*	webhost	Allow, log none
telnet	*	inside_home	Deny, session log
http	*	webhost	Allow, log none
http	*	inside_home	Deny, session log

With Service Groups:

Service	Source	Destination	Type
Webservices	*	webhost	Allow, log none
Webservices	*	inside_home	Deny, session log

Additional services can be created with SunScreen EFS, using one of the predefined state engines (protocols). For example, if you have an ftp implementation that uses port 45 for its control port and port 44 for data, you could define a new ftp service called *ftp-45*. Refer to the product documentation for complete instructions on how to set up an additional service.

Optional Rule Elements

In addition to the basic rule elements discussed in the previous section, there are a variety of optional rule parameters that need to be set, depending on whether or not you are using encryption or proxies.

Proxies

Note – Proxies are not available in SPF-200. Proxy functionality is limited in EFS 2.0. Please refer to the customer documentation for specific details.

Proxies are user-level applications that run on a firewall. The main purpose of a proxy is to provide user authentication and content filtering. SunScreen EFS 2.0 supports four proxies: FTP, SMTP, HTTP, and TELNET. Each proxy, except

TELNET, has specific field value pairs that need to be selected in order for the proxy to function correctly. These are shown in Table 6-3. In addition, both the TELNET and FTP proxies support end-user authentication.

Table 6-3   Proxy Field Value Pairs

	Field Value Pairs	
Proxy	**Command**	**Negative**
FTP	get	no get
	put	no put
	chdir	no chdir
	mkdir	no mkdir
	rename	no rename
	remove dir	no remove_dir
	delete	no delete
SMTP	relay	no relay
HTTP	cookies	no cookies
	Active_X	no active_x
	SSL	no SSL
plus one of the following	java, no java, java signature, java hash, java signature hash	

Encryption

The Encryption parameter tells the SunScreen what kind of encryption to use for the packets described by the other fields in the rule. All encrypted rules are encrypted using SKIP. This parameter has two options: SKIP Version 1 and SKIP Version 2.

SKIP Version 1 is used in the SunScreen SPF-100 and SPF-100G. SKIP Version 2 is a later version of SKIP and is the one currently used in all other SunScreen products. SKIP Version 1 is still an option to allow current SunScreen products to be able to interoperate with the original SPF-100 and SPF-100Gs.

The encryption calculations are based on the certificate for the source and destination machines. All SunScreens must have a certificate. In the example network in Figure 6-1, there are two SunScreens; therefore, you must have two certificates, as shown in the table below.

SunScreen Name	Certificate Name
guard1	guard1cert
guard2	guard2cert

Putting All the Rule Elements Together

In the above sections, the focus has been on individual components, both required and optional, that make up a rule. How do they all fit together? The example rules below show just how straightforward or how complex a rule can be. The diagram in Figure 6-1 is used to define the network. The addresses and address lists are the ones defined in the previous sections.

The first rule is a basic rule:
Allow FTP traffic from anywhere to the FTP server, no logging, no snmp.

This rule translates to:

Source Address	Destination Address	Service	Rule Type, Parameter
* (anywhere)	webhost	FTP	allow, log none, no snmp.

If you want to see where the traffic is coming from, modify the rule to do session logging, which gives you the address of the sender. You can later look up who is using ftp and, hopefully, using your product.

Source Address	Destination Address	Service	Rule Type, Parameter
* (anywhere)	webhost	FTP	allow, log session, no snmp.

If you want only certain people to access this server, you can set up the rule to allow only encrypted traffic. In this case, you will only allow packets that have been encrypted using a certificate from the remote SunScreen (guard2) to have access to the FTP server. This rule is a little more complex, but still logical.

Source Address	Destination Address	Service	Rule Type, Parameter	Encryption Type, Parameter
remote	webhost	FTP	allow, log none, no snmp.	SKIP Version 2, guard2 guard1

If you decide to more closely monitor the incoming ftp traffic from the outside, you may decide to use an FTP proxy server. This time, you want a rule that only allows inbound ftp traffic: users can get files, but not put or delete them; users can change directories, but not create, rename, or remove them. The rule would look like this:

Source Address	Destination Address	Service	Rule Type, Parameter	User	Proxy Type, Parameters
* (anywhere)	webhost	FTP-proxy	allow, log none, no snmp.	anonymous	ftp_proxy, get, no put, chdir, no mkdir, no rename, no remove dir, no delete

To allow a particular person from within the corporate or sales network to administer the FTP proxy server, you would create a rule similar to the one above, but allowing all proxy parameters and adding a field for user authentication.

Source Address	Destination Address	Service	Rule Type, Parameter	User	Proxy Type, Parameters
inside_home	webhost	FTP-proxy	allow, log none, no snmp.	webmaster	ftp_proxy, get, put, chdir, mkdir, rename, remove dir, delete

To prevent someone from "accidentally" ending up on your finance server and releasing your earnings to the world prematurely, you would add a rule that prevents them from trying to ftp to anywhere else inside your network. For

this rule, you want to deny ftp traffic from anywhere to anyplace else, use
summary logging to keep track of who's trying but not send an SNMP trap or
an ICMP message. This rule translates to:

Source Address	Destination Address	Service	Rule Type, Parameter
* (anywhere)	inside_home	FTP	deny, summary log, no snmp, no icmp.

Later, we show you how to enter the rules described in these tables into the
SunScreen EFS or SunScreen SPF-200.

Other Elements That Affect Your Configuration

Some other elements, such as tunneling and SNMP alerts, can affect the rules
but are set globally instead of being set as part of a specific configuration.

Tunneling

Tunneling hides the actual source and destination addresses of encrypted
packets. By using the SunScreen tunneling feature, you can substitute the
addresses on the packet header with another address. These addresses are
usually the addresses of the SunScreen Screens that perform the encryption
and decryption. Tunnelling is usually used for setting up a virtual private
network (VPN).

Tunneling is set on a per certificate basis, and is done where the certificates are
entered. (Certificates tab in the Registry for EFS 2.0; the Registry for SPF-200.)

SNMP Alerts

Simple Network Management Protocol (SNMP) is a common network
management protocol for TCP/IP networks. SunScreen EFS and SPF allow you
to send an SNMP alert when the conditions of a deny rule type are met. The
alert address is set on an interface basis and is set in the Default Action and
SNMP Alert pages on the EFS 2.0.

Turning Your Security Policy into SunScreen Rules

As you have just seen, rules are used to control access to your computer network and to control encryption for access to your data. The SunScreen default is to drop any packets that do not specifically match a rule. This approach makes it easier to create rules, since you only have to write a rule for the services you want to allow or for packets that you want SunScreen to deny but which you want to track in the log file.

In preparing to implement rules, you have:

- Determined the overall services that are available on your network
- Determined the services available to a particular user or host and user groups over particular IP addresses
- Determined the correct action for the service and addresses for that user or host
- Determined the type of encryption (if any) to be used
- Determined what proxies will be used

To create a better example, we modified the network topology map in Figure 6-1 to show a Manufacturing network and an Engineering network. This modified topology map is shown in Figure 6-2. Services, Addresses, and Certificates will be entered via the command line before you create the rules.

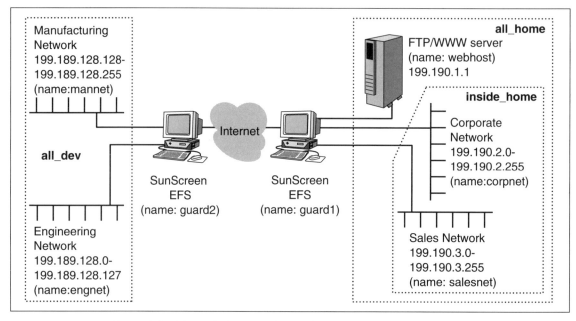

Figure 6-2   Expanded Network Topology Map

The Security Policy has the following conditions:

- There are no restrictions on outbound traffic.
- Traffic between the two SunScreens will always be encrypted.
- Anyone can go to the FTP/WWW server for FTP or HTTP.
- Telnet to anywhere in the network, including the FTP/WWW server, is not allowed.
- The Engineering network can be accessed only by people on the Engineering network.
- Both SunScreens will be locally administered.

The first part of creating rules is to create the rule components. The sections that follow show you how to turn the security policy and network topology into addresses, certificates, and services. The final section shows you how to combine the pieces to create rules.

Creating Address Names

The first step in creating rules is to have all the addresses in the Registry. Later, when you are creating the rules, you will select from the address names you have entered here. Referring back to Figure 6-2 and the security policy, you can create your addresses, address ranges, and address lists, as shown in the tables below.

Address names first:

Network Component	Address Name
FTP/WWW Server	webhost
local SunScreen EFS	localhost
remote SunScreen EFS	guard2

Then, the address ranges:

Network Component	Address Name	Range
Corporate Network	corpnet	199.190.2.0 - 199.190.2.255
Sales Network	salesnet	199.190.3.0 - 199.190.3.255
Engineering Network	engnet	199.189.128.0 - 199.189.128.127
Manufacturing Network	mannet	199.189.128.128 - 199.989.128.255

Finally, the address lists:

Address List Name	Addresses in List
inside_home	corpnet, salesnet
all_home	inside_home, webhost
all_dev	engnet, mannet
all_net	all_dev, all_home

These lists are entered into the SunScreen by means of either the Registry page in the GUI or the command-line interface, as shown below.

```
# ss_address default add "corpnet" NETWORK 199.190.2.0 199.190.2.255 "Corporate Network"
```

Entering Certificates

The Security Policy states that all traffic between all_dev and all_home must be encrypted. This means you must enter the certificates into the SunScreen configuration, using either the Registry or the command-line interface. The certificates for each SunScreen must be transferred to the other SunScreen in a secure fashion. They are then loaded into the respective Screens. Certificates are "global" in that they are not unique to one configuration. An entity can have more than one valid certificate, so when you enter the certificate into the Registry, you give the certificate a unique name.

SunScreen Name	Certificate Name
guard1	guard1cert
guard2	guard2cert

For this policy, you will be entering certificates for both SunScreens, using either the Registry or the command-line interface, as shown below.

```
# ss_certificate add "guardcert" CERTIFICATE 1 0x12345678 SUNSCREEN "" ""
```

Creating a Service Group

Most of the time, you will not need to create a new individual service but you can greatly reduce the number of rules in your configurations by creating Service

Groups. The Security Policy allows you to take advantage of this feature by creating a Service Group for the FTP and WWW services, as shown below.

Service Group Name	Services
webhost_services	http, www

This service group is then entered into the Screen via the Services tab in the Registry or by using the command-line interface, as shown below.

```
# ss_service default add "webhost_services" GROUP {ftp www} "webhost services"
```

Creating the Rules

Now that you have finished defining the components of the rule that you will be using, you can start to create the rules. In this section, each statement in the Security Policy is turned into one or more rules, using the components you just defined. To keep matters simple, you will create the configuration for SunScreen guard1, except for the rules about the Engineering network.

There are no restrictions on outbound traffic.

This rule takes care of the outbound traffic from the network. Notice that the source is inside_home and not all_home. Using inside_home prevents anyone from initiating traffic on webhost. If you want to be more specific on what you want to allow outbound, you would make a service group containing the services you specifically want to allow.

Source Address	Destination Address	Service	Rule Type, Parameter
inside_home	*	common_services	allow, log none, no snmp.

The version for the guard2 configuration would use all_dev instead of inside_home.

Traffic between the two SunScreens will always be encrypted.

This is another basic rule. But, since encryption is one-way, you have to create a rule encrypting in each direction.

Source Address	Destination Address	Service	Rule Type, Parameter	Encryption Type, Parameter
all_dev	all_home	ip-tunnel	allow, log none, no snmp	SKIP Version 2, certificate name: guard2cert
all_home	all_dev	ip-tunnel*	allow, log none, no snmp	SKIP Version 2, certificate name: guard1cert

By encrypting the traffic between the two networks, you can let the people in all_dev access information on the FTP/WWW server that outsiders may not have access to.

Anyone can go to the FTP/WWW server for FTP or HTTP.

This rule has a hidden inverse rule: Unless otherwise specified, you can't go anywhere else in the network for FTP/WWW services. We need to write two rules to execute this statement from the Security Policy. We will revisit this rule when we talk about Rule Ordering later in the chapter. Notice that you are using the service group webhost_services to shorten the number of rules you need to write. Note also that you are using inside_home instead of all_home.

Source Address	Destination Address	Service	Rule Type, Parameter
*	webhost	webhost_services	allow, log none, no snmp.
*	inside_home	webhost_services	deny, no log, no snmp, icmp: host forbidden

This rule is not applicable to guard2 since guard2 does not have an FTP server.

Telnet to anywhere in the network, including the FTP/WWW server, is not allowed.

This rule is an example of a blanket deny. By making the icmp type NONE, nothing is sent back to the host. For all intents and purposes, the packets went to a nonexistent address and were simply ignored.

Source Address	Destination Address	Service	Rule Type, Parameter
*	all_net	TELNET	deny, no log, no snmp, icmp: NONE

The Engineering network can be accessed only by people on the Engineering network.

For this rule, the Security Policy could be more clear. Is just dropping the packets all right, or do you want to keep track of who's trying to get into this network? The rule below is written to keep a log of everyone who tries to get into engnet.

Source Address	Destination Address	Service	Rule Type, Parameter
*	engnet	ip-all	deny, session log, no icmp

Both SunScreens will be locally administered.

Sometimes, things that sound like rules don't require any rule after all. If you were to remotely administer one or the other EFSes, then you would exchange certificates with the remote machine, but in this case, there is no need to create a special rule. To add additional administrators, however, you need to use either the Administrative Access Rules page in EFS or the command line.

Entering a Rule in SunScreen EFS

Rules can be entered in the SunScreen EFS through either the Configuration page (Figure 6-3) or the `ss_rule` command, as shown below.

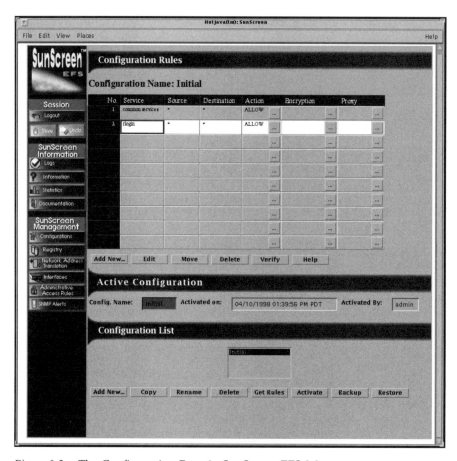

Figure 6-3   The Configuration Page in SunScreen EFS 2.0

```
# ss_rule default Initial add inside_home "*" "common services" ALLOW (LOG_NONE SNMP_NONE)
```

Command-line interface commands can also be entered into a file and then the file can be sourced (in csh) to execute each command in sequence.

How Rules Are Processed

In SunScreen EFS 2.0, rules are processed according to the order in which you put them. In SunScreen SPF-200, rules are processed in a fixed order: encrypted, pass, fail. Both versions require some thinking before you start to enter rules.

Rule Ordering for EFS 2.0

SunScreen EFS 2.0 supports ordered rules. This means that the packet is compared to each rule in order, regardless of the rule type. The packet is then processed according to the parameters of the first exactly matching rule. If none of the rules match, then the rule is processed according to the default action for the interface upon which the packet arrived.

For example, look again at the WWW rules you created in the previous section.

Source Address	Destination Address	Service	Rule Type, Parameter
*	webhost	webhost_services	allow, log none, no snmp.
*	inside_home	webhost_services	deny, no log, no snmp, icmp: host forbidden

Now, let's suppose someone from the sales network wants to go to the WWW server. The way they are ordered now, the first rule (from anywhere to the webhost server - allow) would apply. If, however, you reversed the order of the rules, so that the deny rule was first, then the deny rule would apply and the person from the sales network could not get to the WWW server.

There are two ways to avoid this problem:

1. Be very careful about how you order the rules.

2. Create an address group that consists of "not" all_home and all_dev. Call this address group "outside"; it would replace the asterisk (*) "anywhere" in the rules where you really meant "anywhere that is not inside our network." The advantage here is that there is no ambiguity about who is allowed or not allowed.

The rules you wrote earlier would then become:

Source Address	Destination Address	Service	Rule Type, Parameter
*	webhost	webhost_services	allow, log none, no snmp.
outside	inside_home	webhost_services	deny, no log, no snmp, icmp: host forbidden

You still use the asterisk (*) to represent anywhere, since that is what you really mean in the first rule. The second asterisk (*) has been replaced by the address group outside, making it no longer a match for the all_home or dev_net networks.

Rule Ordering in SPF-200 1.0

SunScreen SPF-200s use a different method of evaluating rules. The packet is evaluated first against all the SKIP rules, then all the Pass rules, then all the Deny rules. If there is no match, the rule is processed according to the default action for the interface upon which the packet arrived.

Reviewing Your Current Rules

Access that you allow your users will likely be thoroughly tested by your users. In fact, there may be things that they have been doing that you were not aware of and they are no longer able to do. You will have to decide on a case-by-case basis whether you are will allow them to continue in their ways.

For example, you might have inadvertently forgotten to allow your users World Wide Web access. In this case, you can simply add it to the "allowed outbound" service. Or, a small group of users might need access to a particular network service, but you don't want every user to have that access. In this case, you would create a separate address list that only includes the hosts of those specific users and a separate rule that only allows that set of addresses to use the particular service.

Often, you may have users who have Internet access outside your organization. Ask them to determine whether they can browse your web site, send you email, and ftp files. If they can't get in, then you will need to modify your configuration to allow WWW, SMTP, and ftp services inbound.

A much harder and as yet unsolved problem is how to ensure or even check that things you don't want to happen can't happen.

Increasing the Effectiveness of Your Rules

This section provides some suggestions on increasing the effectiveness of your rules.

Rules to Help Protect Against Denial-of-Service Attacks

Although there is no foolproof way to deal with SYN flooding[1], a few things tend to minimize it. The primary issue is to limit the set of legitimate source addresses to those which are really necessary. This approach leaves the would-be assailant to guess which addresses will make it through the Screen, thus limiting the assailant's opportunity to deploy those as source addresses. In addition, the assailant must guess the set of destination hosts that will accept these source addresses. Obviously, a few of the hosts in many environments are targets: public web servers and DNS servers are normally required to be open to all comers.

Avoid using the EFS itself for published services; this avoidance will protect the EFS itself from assault.

IP Spoofing

Obviously, for critical traffic among cooperative peers, use of SKIP can provide authentication of such traffic.

The EFS can have its interface definition augmented to provide a measure of anti-spoofing by defining the sets of addresses that can legitimately appear as source on each interface. This technique can prevent the Screen from passing traffic which cannot possibly be correct. Such blocks are commonly placed in routers also.

---

1. SYN flooding is a denial-of-service attack that overloads a system with a flood of connection requests, all with forged source addresses.

An important reason to configure the interface address features is the containment of damage, should an attack succeed. If a hacker can gain access to a system behind the SunScreen, it is still possible to restrict the number of hosts the hacked system can pretend to be.

Tips to Increase Performance

On SunScreen EFS 2.0, you can optimize your rules by placing those that address the highest volume of network traffic earlier in your list so they are considered first. Specific rules should also be placed before general rules, to be sure that they will be executed.

You can also keep down the amount of irrelevant traffic by creating an address group of "bad" addresses and then defining an address group, called "outside," that consists of everything not bad. By using the outside address instead of *, you can respond quickly to get rid of the IP addresses that send junk mail or are repeat offenders for trying to break in. Placing this rule first gets rid of the junk before it has a chance to be allowed by another rule.

Summary

Below is the full configuration of the policy we described earlier for the network shown in Figure 6-2 on page 84. Note that the addresses section defines each port for the two SunScreens, in addition to the single hosts for the web server. Because this is a real configuration, it also defines the routers. The rules have been enhanced and ordered according to several of the tips in the performance section.

```
##########
# addresses

ss_address default add guard1-le0 HOST 199.190.1.15 \
        "guard1-FTP/WWW server network"
ss_address default add guard1-qe0 HOST 199.190.2.15 \
        "guard1-Corporate Network"
ss_address default add guard1-qe1 HOST 199.190.3.15 \
        "guard1-Sales Network"
```

```
ss_address default add guard1-qe2 HOST 199.190.4.15 \
          "guard1-internet"
ss_address default add guard2-le0 HOST 199.189.128.129 \
          "guard2-Manufacturing Network"
ss_address default add guard2-qe0 HOST 199.189.128.89 \
          "guard2-internet"
ss_address default add guard2-qe1 HOST 199.189.128.90 \
          "guard2-Engineering Network"
ss_address default add router1 HOST 199.190.1.254 "router-site1"
ss_address default add router2 HOST 199.189.128.254 "router-site2"
ss_address default add webnet HOST 199.190.4.1 "FTP, WWW server"


ss_address default add guard1_all LIST { \
          guard1-le0 guard1-qe0 guard1-qe1 guard1-qe2 } { } \
          "SunScreen EFS - site1 - all interfaces"
ss_address default add guard2_all LIST { \
          guard2-le0 guard2-qe0 guard2-qe1 } { } \
          "SunScreen EFS - site2 - all interfaces"
ss_address default add all_screens LIST { guard1_all guard2_all } { } \
          "all SunScreen EFSes"
ss_address default add routers_site1 LIST { router1 guard1_all } { } \
          "all routers at site1"
ss_address default add routers_site2 LIST { router2 guard2_all } { } \
          "all routers at site2"


ss_address default add corpnet RANGE 199.190.2.0 199.190.2.255 \
          "corporate network"
ss_address default add salesnet RANGE 199.190.3.0 199.190.3.255 \
          "sales network"
ss_address default add engnet RANGE 199.189.128.0 199.189.128.127 \
          "engineering network"
ss_address default add mannet RANGE 199.189.128.128 199.189.128.255 \
          "manufacturing network"


ss_address default add inside_home LIST \
          { corpnet salesnet } { all_screens } \
          "corporate and sales networks, less EFSes"
```

```
ss_address default add all_home LIST \
          { inside_home webnet } { all_screens } \
          "all controlled nodes at site 1, less EFSes"
ss_address default add all_dev LIST { engnet mannet } { all_screens }
          "all controlled nodes at site 2, less EFSes"
ss_address default add all_net LIST { all_dev all_home } { all_screens } \
          "all controlled nodes at all sites, less EFSes"


ss_address default add bad1 HOST 223.255.255.254 "illegal address"
ss_address default add bad LIST { bad1 } { } "illegal addresses"
ss_address default add any LIST { } { bad } "allowed addresses"


ss_address default add outside LIST { any } { all_net } \
          "all nodes outside SunScreen control"


##############
# certificates


ss_certificate add guard1cert 8 0x111122223333444455556666677778888 \
          SUNSCREEN 199.190.1.15 "" "guard1 - udh"
ss_certificate add guard2cert 8 0x22223333444455556666777788889999 \
          SUNSCREEN 199.189.128.129 "" "guard2 - udh"


###############
# service groups


ss_services default efs-services GROUP { dns "icmp all" ping } \
          "services that the EFSes can do outbound"
ss_service default internal_services GROUP { "tcp all" "udp all" \
          syslog dns "icmp all" ftp rsh archie traceroute ping \
          "rpc all" "nfs prog" "real audio" pmap udp all" "pmap tcp all" \
          "rpc tcp all" nis } \
          "services allowed within"
ss_service default outbound_services GROUP { "tcp all" "udp all" \
          syslog dns "icmp all" ftp rsh archie traceroute ping } \
          "services allowed outbound"
ss_service default webnet_services GROUP { ftp www } \
          "services allowed inbound to webnet"
```

```
#######
# rules


# 1- deny illegal source traffic
ss_rule default guard1 add "ip all" bad "*" \
          DENY ( LOG_NONE SNMP_NONE ICMP_NONE )


# 2- provide proper routing information
ss_rule default guard1 add rip routers_site1 routers_site1 \
          ALLOW ( LOG_NONE SNMP_NONE )

ss_rule default guard1 add rip routers_site1 all_home \
          ALLOW ( LOG_NONE SNMP_NONE )


# 3- provide selected outbound services from SunScreen EFSes
ss_rule default guard1 add efs-services guard1_all all_home \
          ALLOW ( LOG_NONE SNMP_NONE )

ss_rule default guard1 add efs-services guard1_all outside \
          ALLOW ( LOG_NONE SNMP_NONE )


# 4- deny all other access to the SunScreen EFSes
ss_rule default guard1 add "ip all" * all_screens \
          DENY ( LOG_NONE SNMP_NONE ICMP_NONE )


# 5- deny all usage of telnet
ss_rule default guard1 add telnet * "*" \
          DENY ( LOG_NONE SNMP_NONE ICMP_NONE )


# 6- allow site2 hosts to talk encrypted to all (site1) home hosts
ss_rule default guard1 add internal_services all_dev all_home \
          SKIP_VERSION_2 ( guard2cert guard1cert DES-CBC RC4 MD5 ) \
          ALLOW ( LOG_NONE SNMP_NONE )


# 7- allow (site1) home hosts to talk encrypted only to (site2) mannet hosts
ss_rule default guard1 add internal_services all_home mannet \
          SKIP_VERSION_2 ( guard1cert guard2cert DES-CBC RC4 MD5 ) \
          ALLOW ( LOG_NONE SNMP_NONE )
```

```
# 8- allow all outbound traffic
ss_rule default guard1 add outbound_services inside_home any \
        ALLOW ( LOG_NONE SNMP_NONE )


# 9- allow published services in-the-clear
ss_rule default guard1 add webnet_services any webnet \
        ALLOW ( LOG_NONE SNMP_NONE )


# 10- trap any other attempts into engineering
ss_rule default guard1 add "ip all" any engnet \
        DENY ( LOG_DETAIL SNMP_NONE ICMP_NONE )


# 11- ensure all other internal traffic is denied
ss_rule default guard1 add "ip all" all_net all_net \
        DENY ( LOG_NONE SNMP_NONE ICMP_NONE )
```

Scenarios with the SunScreen EFS Firewall A

This appendix describes five scenarios that use the SunScreen EFS firewall. This appendix only shows examples of implementation; it is not meant to suggest a model for all networks nor to design a security policy and rules.

Each scenario includes a diagram, a discussion, and sample rules. In the rules section, each rule in the table represents a translation from the organization's security policy; this information is typically found in the "Standards" section of the policy. The rule sets are examples only and are not meant to be complete and comprehensive.

A

Scenario: Perimeter Defense

Diagram

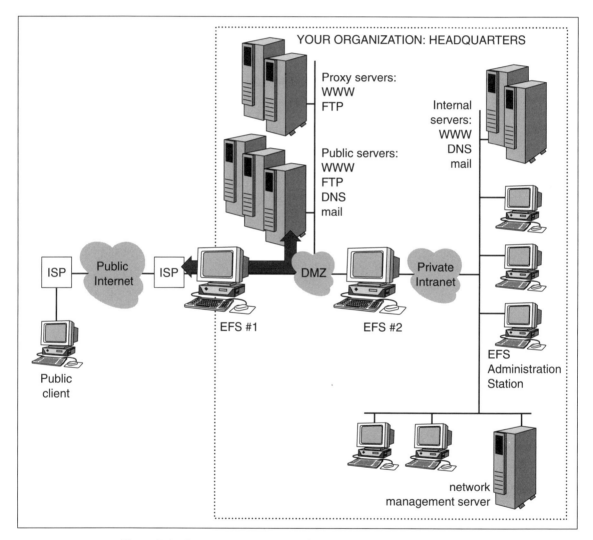

Figure A-1   Scenario: Perimeter Defense

Discussion

In this scenario, the goal is perimeter defense. This scenario is set up to:

1. Provide the initial defense between the public Internet and your organization's private intranet

2. Provide public access to your organization's web-based information through the public Internet

This scenario emphasizes rules for the perimeter firewall, SunScreen EFS #1. The SunScreen EFS #1 firewall is situated between the public Internet and the organization's DMZ network. (The DMZ acts as a kind of buffer area between the Internet and your private networks.) The main role of SunScreen EFS #1 is to act as the initial defense between the public Internet and the private intranet.

No traffic is allowed directly between the public Internet and the systems beyond the DMZ. All traffic coming from the public Internet must first pass through a DMZ-based server before it is sent to the private intranet. No traffic from the private Intranet is allowed to pass straight into the public Internet.

Because you have little control over packets arriving at EFS #1 from the Internet, the data collected in the log file for dropped packets varies greatly. Session-oriented logs generated on the firewall may be helpful in tracking internal users accessing the public Internet. These session-oriented logs may augment accounting information generated by the DMZ-based proxy servers.

A

Rules

Service	Source	Destination	Encryption	Description of Rule
http	public Internet	DMZ public web server	no	allow public users to access your public web site
ftp	public Internet	DMZ public FTP server	no	allow public users to upload and download files to and from your public FTP server
smtp	public Internet	DMZ public mail server	no	allow public users to send mail to your organization's internal mail systems, using the DMZ mail server
dns	public Internet	DMZ public DNS server	no	allow public DNS servers to query the public name database on the DMZ DNS server
http	DMZ web proxy server	public Internet	no	allow your internal users at headquarters to surf the public Internet, using the DMZ web proxy server
ftp	DMZ FTP proxy server	public Internet	no	allow your internal users at headquarters to use FTP to exchange files with the public Internet, using the DMZ FTP proxy server
smtp	DMZ mail server	public Internet	no	allow your internal users at headquarters to send mail to the public Internet, using the DMZ mail server
dns	DMZ DNS server	public Internet	no	allow your DNS server at headquarters to resolve Internet host names, using the DMZ DNS server

snmp	network management server	EFS #1 firewall	no	allow remote management of your EFS firewall
rlogin	system administrator's workstations	EFS #1 firewall	yes	allow system administrator's workstations to securely administer the machine on which the EFS firewall is installed
EFS admin traffic	EFS Administration Station	EFS #1 firewall	yes	allow EFS administrators full privileges on the EFS #1 firewall. (Set on the Administrative Access Rules page.)

Additional rules depending on your organization's security policy

Scenario: Two Lines of Defense

Diagram

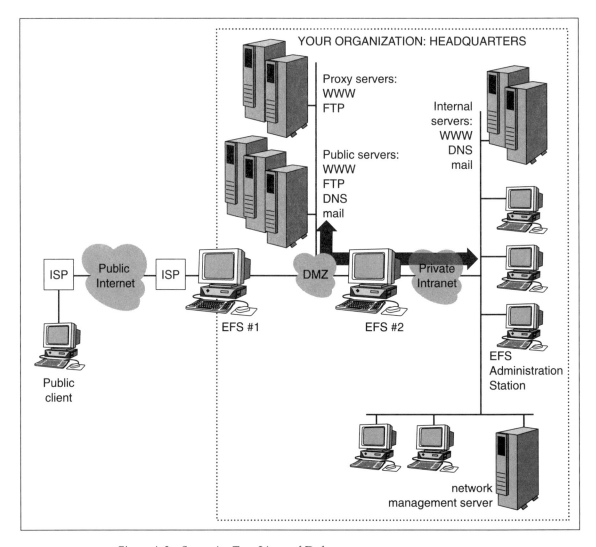

Figure A-2 Scenario: Two Lines of Defense

Discussion

This scenario builds on the previous perimeter defense scenario and is set up to:

1. Provide two layers of defense between the public Internet and your organization's private intranet

2. Provide public access to your organization's web-based information through the public Internet

This scenario emphasizes the rules for the internal firewall, SunScreen EFS #2, that protects the private intranet from public users. The main role of SunScreen EFS #2 is to act as an additional defense between the public Internet and the private intranet.

No traffic is allowed directly between the public Internet and the systems in the private intranet. All traffic coming from the private intranet must first pass through a DMZ proxy server before it is sent to the public Internet. No traffic from the public Internet is allowed to pass straight into the private intranet. Mail is allowed in to the private intranet from the DMZ mail server, so make sure that the DMZ mail server itself is secured.

Because the SunScreen EFS #1 perimeter firewall is already filtering "bad" packets coming from the Internet and because your internal network presumably is not producing a large amount of "bad" packets, the log file on the SunScreen EFS #2 firewall for dropped packets should be more predictable than the highly variable log data on the SunScreen EFS #1 firewall.

A

Rules

Service	Source	Destination	Encryption	Description of Rule
http	private intranet	DMZ web proxy server	no	allow your internal users at headquarters to access the public Internet, using the DMZ web proxy server
ftp	private intranet	DMZ FTP proxy server	no	allow your internal users at headquarters to use FTP to exchange files with the public Internet, using the DMZ FTP proxy server
smtp	DMZ mail server	private intranet mail server	no	allow DMZ mail server to forward mail received from the public Internet to your organization's mail server inside the private intranet
dns	DNS internal server	DMZ public DNS server	no	allow DNS server in private intranet to query public DNS server in the DMZ; the DMZ DNS server can then query a DNS server on the public Internet
rlogin	system administrator's workstations	DMZ servers	yes	allow system administrator's workstations to securely access DMZ servers
snmp	network management server	DMZ servers	no	allow server to remotely manage all devices in the DMZ
snmp	network management server	EFS #2 firewall	no	allow remote management of your EFS firewall

Computer Security Policies and SunScreen Firewalls

rlogin	system administrator's workstations	EFS #2 firewall	yes	allow system administrator's workstations to securely administer the machine on which the EFS firewall is installed
EFS admin traffic	EFS Administration Station	EFS #2 firewall	yes	allow EFS administrators full privileges on the EFS #2 firewall. (Set on the Administrative Access Rules page.)

Additional rules depending on your organization's security policy

Scenario: Site-to-Site Tunneling Firewall

Diagram

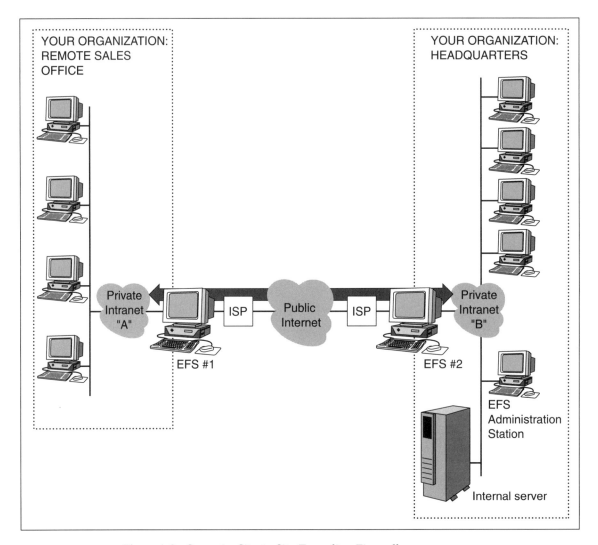

Figure A-3   Scenario: Site-to-Site Tunneling Firewall

Discussion

This scenario is set up to support site-to-site encrypted tunnels across the public Internet.

In this scenario, a SunScreen EFS firewall is situated between the public Internet and the private intranet at the organization's headquarters. The main role of this firewall is to act as an end point for encrypted tunnels established between the corporate network at headquarters and a remote sales office over the public Internet.

All IP traffic exchanged between the sites is encrypted regardless of the service type. Other than the encrypted traffic between the specified sites and support for administrative access to the SunScreen EFS firewall, no other IP traffic is allowed into or through the EFS firewall system at headquarters.

Rules

Service	Source	Destination	Encryption	Description of Rule
all (ip tunnel)	private Internal network "A"	private Internal network "B"	yes	allow encrypted, bidirectional channel between your remote sales office and headquarters
snmp	network management server	EFS firewall	no	allow remote management of your EFS firewall
rlogin	system administrator's workstations	EFS firewall	yes	allow system administrator's workstations to securely administer the machine on which the EFS firewall is installed

Additional rules depending on your organization's security policy

Scenario: Remote Access Firewall

Diagram

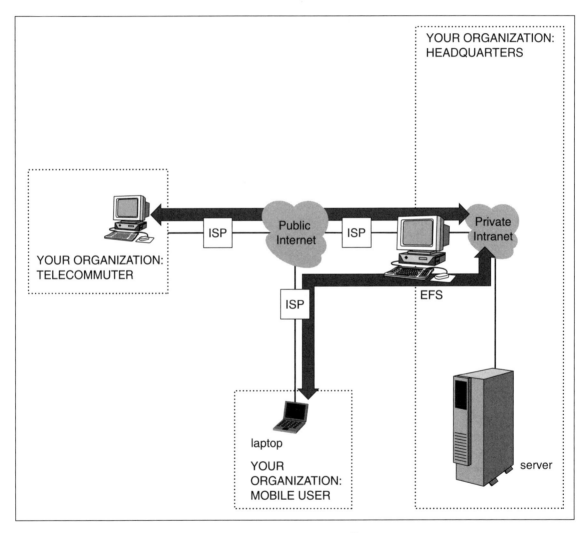

Figure A-4   Scenario: Remote Access Firewall

Discussion

This scenario is set up to support telecommuters and mobile users on the Internet. The main role of the firewall is to support encrypted connections between remote users and headquarters over the Internet. The remote users do not necessarily have fixed IP addresses.

Because the IP addresses are not fixed, the remote user must initiate the connection. The Screen authenticates the remote user's SKIP identity and allows or denies the packets based on the parameters in the rule with ip mobile. The Screen also binds the remote user's SKIP identity with his current IP address, so packets can be sent encrypted to him.

Rules

Service	Source	Destination	Encryption	Description of Rule
all (ip mobile)	lists of address ranges	private internal network	yes	allow encrypted channel between remote users and the organization's private internal network over the public Internet
snmp	network management server	EFS firewall	no	allow remote management of your EFS firewall
rlogin	system administrator's workstations	EFS firewall	yes	allow system administrator's workstations to securely administer the machine on which the EFS firewall is installed

Additional rules depending on your organization's security policy

Scenario: Compartmentalization Firewall

Diagram

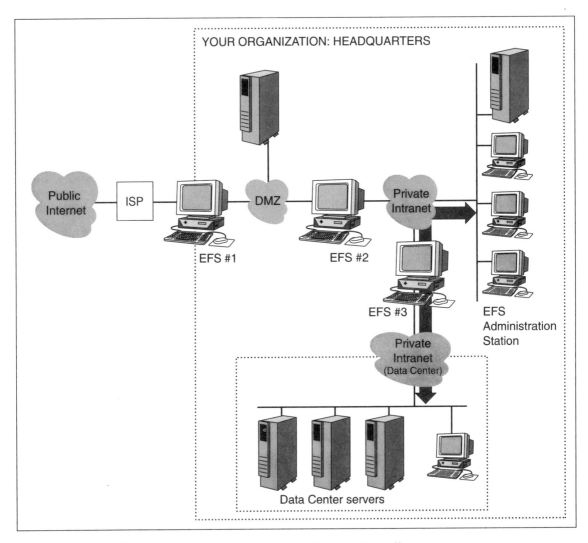

Figure A-5 Scenario: Compartmentalization Firewall

Discussion

This scenario is set up to provide compartmentalization within a private intranet. The SunScreen EFS #3 firewall is situated between two internal networks. The "Data Center" network contains servers that must be up and running 24 hours a day, 7 days a week. The organization can't allow general access to this environment (unlike to a workgroup server); the access needs to be controlled.

Another reason to compartmentalize might be to keep sensitive data separate; this information could include financial data or personnel data, for example.

Rules

Service	Source	Destination	Encryption	Description of Rule
snmp	network management server	Data Center network and EFS #3	no	allow remote management of devices in the Data Center network
dns	Data Center network	Internal DNS servers	no	allow Data Center servers to resolve host names other than local hosts
rlogin	system administrator workstations	Data Center network	yes	allow system administrator workstations to securely administer Data Center systems
rlogin	system administrator's workstations	EFS firewall	yes	allow system administrator's workstations to securely administer the machine on which the EFS firewall is installed
EFS admin traffic	EFS Administration Station	EFS #3 firewall	yes	allow EFS administrators full privileges on the EFS #3 firewall. (Set on the Administrative Access Rules page.)

Additional rules depending on your organization's security policy

Resources

This appendix identifies various sources of information on security, security policies, firewalls, and the SunScreen firewalls.

Resources on the Internet

Request for Comments (RFCs)

- RFC 1825: "Security Architecture for the Internet Protocol"
- RFC 1244: "Site Security Handbook"
- RFC 1700: "Assigned Numbers"

An index of RFCs is located at http://www.ds.internic.net/ds/rfc-index.html.

Web URLs

These World Wide Web uniform resource locators (URLs) provide background and up-to-date information on security. The URLs were current as of this book's publication date.

- Computer Emergency Response Team (CERT), http://www.cert.org/
- Forum of Incident Response and Security Teams (FIRST),
  http://www.first.org/
- U.S. Department of Energy's Computer Incident Advisory Capability
  (CIAC), http://www.ciac.llnl.gov/

- U.S. National Institute of Standards and Technology (NIST), http://www.csrc.nist.gov/
- Computer Operations, Audit, and Security Technology (COAST), http://www.cs.purdue.edu/coast/
- Computer Security Institute (CSI), http://www.gocsi.com/

Internet Newsgroups

These Usenet newsgroups provide information and discussion on security and firewalls:

- comp.risks
- comp.security
- comp.security.announce
- comp.security.firewalls
- comp.unix.security

Books

Chapman, D. Brent, and Elizabeth D. Zwicky, *Building Internet Firewalls*, O'Reilly & Associates, Inc. (1995) ISBN 1-56592-124-0

Cheswick, William, and Steve Bellovin, *Firewalls and Internet Security*, Addison-Wesley (Reading, MA, 1994) ISBN 0-201-63357-4

Garfinkel, Simson, and Gene Spafford, *Practical UNIX and Internet Security*, O'Reilly & Associates, Inc. (Sebastopol, CA, 1995) ISBN 1-56592-148-8

Kaufman, Charlie, Radia Perlman, and Mike Speciner, *Network Security*, PTR Prentice Hall (Englewood Cliffs, NJ, 1995) ISBN 0-13-061466-1

SunScreen Product Documentation

The SunScreen EFS 2.0 documentation includes:

- *SunScreen EFS Installation Guide*
- *SunScreen EFS Administration Guide*
- *SunScreen EFS Reference Manual*

The SunScreen SPF-200 1.0 documentation includes:

- *SunScreen SPF-200 Installation Guide*

- *SunScreen SPF-200 Configuration and Management Guide*

The SunDocs™ program provides more than 250 manuals from Sun Microsystems, Inc. If you live in the United States, Canada, Europe, or Japan, you can purchase documentation sets or individual manuals through this program.

For a list of documents and how to order them, see the catalog section of the SunExpress™ Internet site at http://www.sun.com/sunexpress.

Index

F

file
   log file, 16, 17, 65, 70
   permissions, 32
firewall, defined, 19
FTP, 12, 28, 57, 65, 66, 78, 79

G

GUI, 52, 56

H

help, *see* monitoring; troubleshooting
high availability, 57
HTTP, 12, 22, 57, 69, 79

I

ICMP data, 77
information classification, 12
integrity, 32
interface, 44, 49, 58, 60
Internet, defined, 2
intranet, defined, 2
IP, 60
IP address, 21, 26, 27, 57, 60, 71, 73 to 74, 75
IP spoofing, 93
ISP, 27, 54

K

key technology, 33 to 39

L

log browser, 67
log file, 16, 17, 65, 70

M

management, obtaining support of, 8
MIB, 68
mission statement, 7

monitoring, 17, 65 to 68

N

naming services, 69
NAT, 27, 46, 72
network address, 42, 49
network address translation, *see* NAT
network management station, 72
network services, 12, 51, 57, 77 to 78
network topology map, 72
NFS, 24

O

Orange Book, 4

P

packet
   broadcast, 61
   filtering, 21 to 26, 44 to 47
   logging, 66 to 67
password, 13, 56, 58
performance, 46, 47, 66, 94
PFL engine, 46
ping command, 66, 68, 70
port number, 22, 53
privacy, 26, 32
protocol, network, 23
      See also CDP, FTP, HTTP, IP, SMTP, SNMP, TCP,
         UDP
proxy, 25 to 26, 57, 78 to 79

R

random number generator, 62
Registry, 76, 82, 85, 86, 87
RFCs, 115
risk analysis, 5, 8 to 9
router, 72
routing services, 69

CORE JAVA 1.1
Volume I: Fundamentals

**CAY S. HORSTMANN and
GARY CORNELL**

628 pages; (includes CD-ROM)
ISBN 0-13-766957-7

Now in its third revision, CORE JAVA is still the leading Java book for software developers who want to put Java to work on real problems. Written for experienced programmers with a solid background in languages ranging from Visual Basic to COBOL to C and C++, CORE JAVA 1.1, VOLUME 1 concentrates on the underlying Java 1.1 language along with the fundamentals of using the cross-platform graphics library supplied with the JDK™ 1.1.

This must-have reference features comprehensive coverage of the essentials for serious programmers:
- Encapsulation
- Classes and methods
- Inheritance
- The Java 1.1 event model
- Data structures
- Exception handling

The accompanying CD is packed with sample programs that demonstrate key language and library features — no toy code! The CD also includes the Windows 95/NT and Solaris™ versions of the JDK 1.1 and shareware versions of WinEdit, WinZip and TextPad for Windows95/NT.

CORE JAVA 1.1
Volume II: Advanced Features

**CAY S. HORSTMANN and
GARY CORNELL**

630 pages; (includes CD-ROM)
ISBN 0-13-766965-8

For programmers already familiar with the core features of the JAVA 1.1 language, VOLUME 2: ADVANCED FEATURES includes detailed and up-to-date explanations of topics such as:
- Streams
- Multithreading
- Network programming
- JDBC, RMI, JavaBeans™
- Distributed objects

The accompanying CD includes useful sample programs (no toy code!), Windows 95/NT and Solaris™ versions of JDK 1.1, and shareware versions of WinEdit, TextPad, and WinZip.

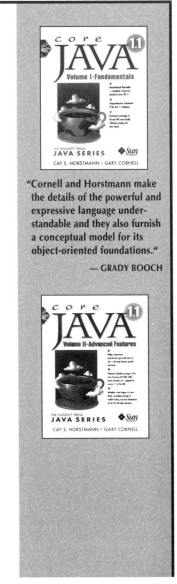

"Cornell and Horstmann make the details of the powerful and expressive language understandable and they also furnish a conceptual model for its object-oriented foundations."

— GRADY BOOCH

GRAPHIC JAVA 1.2
Volume I—Mastering the JFC, Third Edition
DAVID M. GEARY

850 pages; (includes CD-ROM)
ISBN: 0130796662

Written for experienced programmers
looking for thorough and detailed explanations of the 1.2 AWT class libraries,
Volume 1 covers all aspects of the AWT.
It also includes coverage of advanced
topics such as clipboard and data transfer,
double buffering, custom dialogs, and
sprite animation. Focuses heavily on
bringing programmer's up to speed
quickly on the new GUI services like:
• Drag and Drop
• the newest lightweight components
• the delegation event model

JUST JAVA 1.1,
Third Edition
PETER van der LINDEN

652 pages; (includes CD-ROM)
ISBN 0-13-784174-4

In JUST JAVA 1.1, the author of the classic
EXPERT C PROGRAMMING: DEEP C SECRETS
brings his trademark enthusiasm, straight
talk, and expertise to the challenge of learning
Java and object-oriented programming.

In this updated Third Edition, you'll find
all the fundamentals of Java programming,
including Java object-oriented techniques,
types, statements, string processing, as
well as more sophisticated techniques like
networking, threads, and using the Abstract
Window Toolkit. You'll also discover more
examples than ever, along with updated
coverage of future Java APIs—including
the Java Database Connectivity (JDBC) API
completely updated to include coverage
of JDK 1.1.

TOPICS INCLUDE:
• The Story of O—object-oriented
  programming
• Applications versus applets
• Identifiers, comments, keywords, and
  operators
• Arrays, exceptions, and threads
• GIGO—Garbage In, Gospel Out
• On the Internet No One Knows You're
  a Dog

The CD-ROM includes all source code
for examples presented in the book along
with the latest JDK for Solaris, Windows 95,
Windows NT, and Macintosh.

JAVA BY EXAMPLE,
Second Edition

**JERRY R. JACKSON and
ALAN L. McCLELLAN**

380 pages; (includes CD-ROM)
ISBN 0-13-272295-X

There's no better way to learn Java than by example. If you're an experienced programmer, JAVA BY EXAMPLE is the quickest way to learn Java. By reviewing example code written by experts, you'll learn the right way to develop Java applets and applications that are elegant, readable, and easy to maintain.

Step-by-step, working from examples, you'll learn valuable techniques for working with the Java language. The Second Edition provides even more extensive coverage.

TOPICS INCLUDE:

- Memory and constructors
- Input/output
- Multithreading
- Exception handling
- Animation
- Remote methods invocation (RMI)
- Networking
- Java Database Connectivity (JDBC) API

The CD-ROM includes all source code for examples presented in the book along with the JDK for Solaris, Windows 95, Windows NT, and Macintosh.

INSTANT JAVA, Second Edition

JOHN A. PEW

398 pages; (includes CD-ROM)
ISBN 0-13-272287-9

INSTANT JAVA™ applets—no programming necessary! Now anyone can use Java to add animation, sound, and interactivity to their Web pages! Instant Java is your guide to using more than 75 easy-to-customize Java applets. The Second Edition

contains even more applets and examples—plus updated, foolproof instructions for plugging them into your Web pages.

APPLETS INCLUDE:

- Text applets
- Image applets
- Animation applets
- Slide shows
- Tickers

You'll find all the applets on the cross-platform CD-ROM—along with sample HTML pages and the JDK for Solaris,™ Microsoft Windows 95, Microsoft Windows NT, and Macintosh. This is an invaluable tool for adding Java special effects to your HTML documents!

NOT JUST JAVA

PETER van der LINDEN

313 pages; ISBN 0-13-864638-4

NOT JUST JAVA is the book for everybody who needs to understand why Java and other Internet technologies are taking the software industry by storm. Peter van der Linden, author of the best-selling JUST JAVA, carefully explains each of the key technologies driving the Internet revolution and provides a much-needed perspective on critical topics including:
- Java and its libraries—present and future
- Security on intranets and the Internet
- Thin clients, network computers, and webtops
- Multi-tier client/server system
- Software components, objects and CORBA
- The evolution and role of intranets
- JavaBeans™ versus ActiveX

Also included are case studies of leading-edge companies that show how to avoid the pitfalls and how to leverage Java and related technologies for maximum payoff.

"...the most complete and effective treatment of a programming topic since Charles Petzold's classic Programming Windows."

— *COMPUTER SHOPPER*

"Fantastic book/CD package for HTML authors...practical, hands-on instructions get you off to a fast start."

— *COMPUTER BOOK REVIEW*

INSIDE JAVA WORKSHOP 2.0,
2nd Edition
LYNN WEAVER

380 pages; ISBN 0-13-899584-2
(includes CD-ROM)

A guide for new and experienced Java WorkShop users, INSIDE JAVA WORKSHOP 2.0 provides a task-based tour of every tool in the Java development environment from Sun and also highlights how to use the significant new features in version 2.0.

You will quickly learn the basics of the development model, including setting development preferences, building Java projects interactively, analyzing Java program performance, editing code with the enhanced Source Editor,and debugging applets across the Internet. You'll also learn how to use advanced debugging and GUI building features, and how to create, import and deploy JavaBeans projects.

The CD-ROM includes a 30-day, full-functioning version of Java WorkShop along with project examples and sample programs, complete with source code. It also features links to Java resources on the Web.

JUMPING JAVASCRIPT
JANICE WINSOR and BRIAN FREEMAN

1200 pages; (includes CD-ROM)
ISBN 0-13-841941-8

JUMPING JAVASCRIPT™ is a hands-on tutorial with loads of examples that will show both programmers and non-programmers how to use JavaScript to easily incorporate the interactivity of Java into their Web sites. It covers both basics such as scripting concepts, embedded Java applets, image maps, and buttons as well as advanced topics such as creating Java-Script objects and the cookies property. CD-ROM contains all the scripts discussed

in the book.

WEB PAGE DESIGN
A Different Multimedia
MARY E. S. MORRIS and RANDY J. HINRICHS

200 pages; ISBN 0-13-239880-X

Everything you always wanted to know about practical Web page design! Anyone can design a web page, but it takes more than basic HTML skill to build a world-class Web site. Written for Web page authors, this hands-on guide covers the key aspects of designing a successful Web site and shows how to integrate traditional design techniques into Web sites. Contains sixteen full color examples of successful Web pages, and techniques for:

- Cognitive and content design
- Audience consideration
- Interactivity, organization, and navigational pathways
- Designing with VRML and Java
- Working with templates, style sheets, and Netscape™ Frames
- Evolving your design

HTML FOR FUN AND PROFIT,
3rd Edition
MARY E. S. MORRIS and JOHN E. SIMPSON

400 pages; ISBN 0-13-079672-7

The international best seller has been completely revised and updated to feature in-depth coverage of the fundamentals and all the hottest new HTML innovations. You will quickly master using tags, adding hyperlinks, graphics and multimedia, and creating clickable imagemaps. You will also learn the benefits of tables and frames and how to generate pages "on the fly." You will also find information on Dynamic

HTML, cascading style sheets, and XML.

THREADS PRIMER
A Guide to Multithreaded Programming
BIL LEWIS and DANIEL J. BERG

319 pages; ISBN 0-13-443698-9

Written for developers and technical managers, this book provides a solid, basic understanding of threads—what they are, how they work, and why they are useful. It covers the design and implementation of multithreaded programs as well as the business and technical benefits of writing threaded applications.

The THREADS PRIMER discusses four different threading libraries (POSIX, Solaris, OS/2, and Windows NT) and presents in-depth implementation details and examples for the Solaris and POSIX APIs.

PROGRAMMING WITH THREADS
STEVE KLEIMAN, DEVANG SHAH, and BART SMAALDERS

534 pages; ISBN 0-13-172389-8

Multithreaded programming can improve the performance and structure of your applications, allowing you to utilize all the power of today's high performance computer hardware. PROGRAMMING WITH THREADS is the definitive guide to multithreaded programming. It is intended for both novice and experienced threads programmers, with special attention given to the problems of multithreading existing programs. The book provides structured techniques for mastering the complexity of threads programming with an emphasis on performance issues.

TOPICS INCLUDE:

- Synchronization and threading strategies
- Using threads for graphical user interfaces and client-server computing
- Multiprocessors and parallel programming
- Threads implementation and perfor-

mance issues

MULTITHREADED PROGRAMMING WITH PTHREADS
BIL LEWIS and DANIEL J. BERG

382 pages; ISBN 0-13-680729-1

Based on the best-selling THREADS PRIMER, MULTITHREADED PROGRAMMING WITH PTHREADS gives you a solid understanding of Posix threads: what they are, how they work, when to use them, and how to optimize them. It retains the clarity and humor of the Primer, but includes expanded comparisons to Win32 and OS/2 implementations. Code examples tested on all of the major UNIX platforms are featured along with detailed explanations of how and why they use threads. In addition to scheduling, synchronization, signal handling, etc., special emphasis is placed on cancellation, error conditions, performance, hardware, and languages (including Java).

More than anything else this is a practical book—it tells you what can and cannot be done with threads and why. In short, everything you need to know to build faster, smarter, multithreaded applications.

EXPERT C PROGRAMMING:
Deep C Secrets
PETER van der LINDEN

352 pages; ISBN 0-13-177429-8

EXPERT C PROGRAMMING is a very different book on the C language! In an easy, conversational style, the author reveals coding techniques used by the best C programmers. EXPERT C PROGRAMMING explains the difficult areas of ANSI C, from arrays to runtime structures, and all the quirks in between. Covering both IBM PC and UNIX systems, this book is a must read for anyone who wants to learn more about the implementation, practical use, and folklore of C!

CHAPTER TITLES INCLUDE:

- It's not a bug, it's a language feature!
- Thinking of linking
- You know C, so C++ is easy!
- Secrets of programmer job interviews

CONFIGURATION AND CAPACITY PLANNING FOR SOLARIS SERVERS
BRIAN L. WONG

428 pages; ISBN 0-13-349952-9

No matter what application of SPARC architecture you're working with this book can help you maximize the performance of your Solaris-based server. This is the most comprehensive guide to configuring and sizing Solaris servers for virtually any task, including:

* World Wide Web, Internet email, ftp and Usenet news servers * NFS servers
* Database management
* Client/server computing
* Timesharing
* General purpose application servers Internet firewalls

PANIC!
UNIX System Crash Dump Analysis
CHRIS DRAKE and KIMBERLEY BROWN

480 pages; (includes CD-ROM)
ISBN 0-13-149386-8

UNIX systems crash—it's a fact of life. Until now, little information has been available regarding system crashes. PANIC! is the first book to concentrate solely on system crashes and hangs, explaining what triggers them and what to do when they occur. PANIC! guides you through system crash dump postmortem analysis towards problem resolution. PANIC! presents this highly technical and intricate subject in a friendly, easy style that even the novice UNIX system administrator will find readable, educational, and enjoyable.

TOPICS COVERED INCLUDE:

- What is a panic? What is a hang?
- Header files, symbols, and symbol tables
- A comprehensive tutorial on adb, the absolute debugger
- Introduction to assembly language
- Actual case studies of postmortem analysis

A CD-ROM containing several useful analysis tools—such as adb macros and C tags output from the source trees of two different UNIX systems—is included.

SUN PERFORMANCE AND TUNING
Java and the Internet, Second Edition

ADRIAN COCKCROFT and
RICHARD PETTIT

500 pages; ISBN 0-13-095249-4

Hailed in its first edition as an indispensable reference for system administrators, SUN PERFORMANCE AND TUNING has been revised and expanded to cover Solaris 2.6, the newest generation of SPARC hardware and the latest Internet and Java server technologies.

Featuring "Quick Tips and Recipes," as well as extensive reference tables, this book is indispensable both for developers who need to design for performance and administrators who need to improve overall system performance.

KEY TOPICS COVERED INCLUDE:

- Web Server Sizing and Performance Management Tools
- Performance Management and Measurement
- Software Performance Engineering
- Kernel Algorithms and Tuning
- Java Application Servers

To get up to speed quickly on critical perfomance issues, this is the one book any Sun administrator, integrator, or developer needs.

WABI 2:
Opening Windows

SCOTT FORDIN and
SUSAN NOLIN

383 pages; ISBN 0-13-461617-0

WABI™ 2: OPENING WINDOWS explains the ins and outs of using Wabi software from Sun Microsystems to install, run, and manage Microsoft Windows applications on UNIX systems. Easy step-by-step instructions, illustrations, and charts guide you through each phase of using Wabi—from getting started to managing printers, drives, and COM ports to getting the most from your specific Windows applications.

AUTOMATING SOLARIS INSTALLATIONS
A Custom Jumpstart Guide

PAUL ANTHONY KASPER and
ALAN L. McCLELLAN

282 pages; (includes a diskette)
ISBN 0-13-312505-X

AUTOMATING SOLARIS INSTALLATIONS describes how to set up "hands-off" Solaris installations for hundreds of SPARC™ and x86 systems. It explains in detail how to configure your site so that when you install Solaris, you simply boot a system and walk away—the software installs automatically! The book also includes a diskette with working shell scripts to automate pre- and post-installation tasks, such as:

- Updating systems with patch releases
- Installing third-party or unbundled software on users' systems
- Saving and restoring system data
- Setting up access to local and remote printers
- Transitioning a system from SunOS™ 4.x to Solaris 2

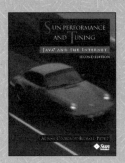

"This book is a must for all Solaris 2 system administrators."
— TOM JOLLANDS,
Sun Enterprise Network Systems

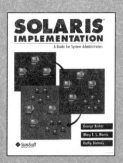

SOLARIS IMPLEMENTATION
A Guide for System Administrators
GEORGE BECKER, MARY E. S. MORRIS, and KATHY SLATTERY

345 pages; ISBN 0-13-353350-6

Written by expert Sun™ system administrators, this book discusses real world, day-to-day Solaris 2 system administration for both new installations and for migration from an installed Solaris 1 base. It presents tested procedures to help system administrators improve and customize their networks and includes advice on managing heterogeneous Solaris environments. Provides actual sample auto install scripts and disk partitioning schemes used at Sun.

TOPICS COVERED INCLUDE:

- Local and network methods for installing Solaris 2 systems
- Configuring with admintool versus command-line processes
- Building and managing the network, including setting up security
- Managing software packages and patches
- Handling disk utilities and archiving procedures

SOLARIS PORTING GUIDE,
Second Edition
SUNSOFT DEVELOPER ENGINEERING

695 pages; ISBN 0-13-443672-5

Ideal for application programmers and software developers, the SOLARIS PORTING GUIDE provides a comprehensive technical overview of the Solaris 2 operating environment and its related migration strategy.

The Second Edition is current through Solaris 2.4 (for both SPARC and x86 platforms) and provides all the information necessary to migrate from Solaris 1 (SunOS 4.x) to Solaris 2 (SunOS 5.x). Other additions include a discussion of emerging technologies such as the Common Desktop Environment from Sun, hints for application performance tuning, and extensive pointers to further information, including Internet sources.

TOPICS COVERED INCLUDE:

- SPARC and x86 architectural differences
- Migrating from common C to ANSI C
- Building device drivers for SPARC and x86 using DDI/DKI
- Multithreading, real-time processing, and the Sun Common Desktop Environment

ALL ABOUT ADMINISTERING NIS+,
Second Edition
RICK RAMSEY

451 pages; ISBN 0-13-309576-2

Take full advantage of your Solaris distributed operating environment by learning how to effectively use the networking power of NIS+ technology. Updated and revised for Solaris 2.3, this book is ideal for network administrators who want to know more about NIS+: its capabilities, requirements, how it works, and how to get the most out of it.

INTERACTIVE UNIX OPERATING SYSTEM
A Guide for System Administrators
MARTY C. STEWART

275 pages; ISBN 0-13-161613-7

Written for first-time system administrators and end users, this practical guide goes step-by-step through the character-based menus for configuring, tailoring, and maintaining the INTERACTIVE™ UNIX® System V/386 Release 3.2, Version 3.0 through Version 4.1. It is also a great reference for any system based on UNIX SVR 3.2.

VERILOG HDL
A Guide to Digital Design and Synthesis
SAMIR PALNITKAR

396 pages; (includes CD-ROM)
ISBN 0-13-451675-3

VERILOG HDL stresses the practical design aspects of using Verilog. Written for both experienced and new users, the guide provides full coverage of gate, dataflow (RTL), behavioral and switch level modeling. The information presented is fully compliant with the upcoming IEEE 1364 Verilog HDL standard.

TOPICS INCLUDE:

- Introduction to the Programming Language Interface (PLI)
- Logic synthesis methodologies
- Timing and delay simulation

The CD-ROM contains a Verilog simulator with a graphical user interface and the source code for the examples in the book.

STEP-BY-STEP ISDN
The Internet Connection Handbook
BEN CATANZARO

308 pages; ISBN 0-13-890211-9

Save time and money! No-hassle strategies for setting up your ISDN Internet connection. Everyone knows ISDN is fast, reliable and powerful. With this book, it's also something you never thought it could be—easy!

STEP-BY-STEP ISDN shows you exactly what to do and what to buy to get a reliable, fast ISDN Internet connection for your business or home office. You'll learn precisely how to prepare your location and computer systems for an ISDN connection, order ISDN service from the telephone company, coordinate ISDN service with your Internet Service Provider, and select the appropriate hardware and software components.

DESIGNING VISUAL INTERFACES
Communication Oriented Techniques
KEVIN MULLET and
DARRELL K. SANO

262 pages; ISBN 0-13-303389-9

DESIGNING VISUAL INTERFACES applies the fundamentals of graphic, industrial, and interior design to solve human/computer interface problems. It describes basic design principles (the what and why), common errors, and practical techniques. Readers will gain a new perspective on product development as well as an appreciation for the contribution visual design can offer to their products and users.

"I highly recommend [this book] to anyone exploring or considering HDL based design."
— BILL FUCHS
CEO, Simucad Inc. and Chairman of the Board of Directors of Open Verilog International (OVI)

"All GUI designers should have this book on their bookshelves."
— MILES O'NEAL,
UNIX Review, January 1996

DEVELOPING VISUAL APPLICATIONS
XIL: An Imaging Foundation Library
WILLIAM K. PRATT

368 pages; ISBN 0-13-461948-X

A practical introduction to using imaging in new, innovative applications for desktop computing. DEVELOPING VISUAL APPLICATIONS breaks down the barriers that prevent developers from easily integrating imaging into their applications. It covers the basics of image processing, compression, and algorithm implementation and provides clear, real-world examples for developing applications using XIL™ a cross-platform imaging foundation library. More experienced imaging developers can also use this book as a reference to the architectural features and capabilities of XIL.

READ ME FIRST!
A Style Guide for the Computer Industry
SUN TECHNICAL PUBLICATIONS

256 pages; (includes CD-ROM)
ISBN 0-13-455347-0

User documentation should be an asset, not an afterthought. The READ ME FIRST! style guide can help technical publications groups outline, organize, and prepare high quality documentation for any type of computer product. Based on the award-winning Sun Microsystems documentation style guide, READ ME FIRST! includes complete guidelines—from style pointers to legal considerations, from writing for an international audience to forming a documentation department.

TOPICS INCLUDE:

- Grammar and punctuation guidelines
- Technical abbreviations, acronyms, and units of measurement
- How to set up your own documentation department

The CD-ROM includes ready-to-use FrameMaker templates for instant page design and the entire book in searchable FrameViewer and HTML format for easy reference.

INTRANET SECURITY:
Stories From the Trenches
LINDA McCARTHY

300 pages; ISBN 0-13-894759-7

Do you have response procedures for systems break-ins? Is your e-mail encrypted? Is your firewall protecting your company? Is your security staff properly trained? These are just a few of the security issues that are covered in INTRANET SECURITY: STORIES FROM THE TRENCHES. Author Linda McCarthy, who in her job as a worldwide security team leader at Sun broke into thousands of corporate intranets, presents detailed case studies of real-life break-ins that will help you make your systems safer. She explains how each breach occurred, describes what steps were taken to fix it, and then provides a practical and systematic solution for preventing similar problems from occurring on your network!

CREATING WORLDWIDE SOFTWARE
Solaris International Developer's Guide, Second Edition

BILL TUTHILL and DAVID SMALLBERG

382 pages; ISBN 0-13-494493-3

A new edition of the essential reference text for creating global applications, with updated information on international markets, standards organizations, and writing international documents. This expanded edition of the Solaris International Developer's Guide includes new chapters on CDE/Motif, NEO/OpenStep, Universal codesets, global internet applications, code examples, and studies of successfully internationalized software.

INTRANETS:
What's the Bottom Line?

RANDY J. HINRICHS

420 pages; ISBN 0-13-841198-0

INTRANETS: WHAT'S THE BOTTOM LINE? is for decisions makers, who want bottom line information in order to figure out what an intranet is and how it will help their organizations. It's a compelling case for the corporate intranet. This book will give you a high-level perspective on intranets and will answer your questions: What is an intranet? What is it made of? What does it buy me? How much does it cost? How do I make it work? How do I know it's working?

HANDS-ON INTRANETS
VASANTHAN S. DASAN and LUIS R. ORDORICA

326 pages; ISBN 0-13-857608-4

This hands-on guide will show you how to implement a corporate intranet, or a private network comprised of the open, standards-based protocols and services of the internet. IS professionals and others interested in implementing an Intranet will learn the key intranet protocols, services, and applications. The book also describes the technical issues such as security, privacy, and other problems areas encountered in intranet implementation and integration, while providing practical solutions for each of these areas. You will learn how to realize the intranet's potential.

RIGHTSIZING FOR CORPORATE SURVIVAL
An IS Manager's Guide

ROBERT MASSOUDI, ASTRID JULIENNE, BOB MILLRADT, and REED HORNBERGER

250 pages; ISBN 0-13-123126-X

Information systems (IS) managers will find hands-on guidance to developing a rightsizing strategy and plan in this fact-filled reference book. Based upon research conducted through customer visits with multinational corporations, it details the experiences and insights gained by IS professionals who have implemented systems in distributed, client/server environments. Throughout the book, case studies and "lessons learned" reinforce the discussion and document best practices associated with rightsizing.

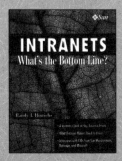

"A great reference tool for IS managers planning rightsizing projects."

— G. PHIL CLARK, Kodak Imaging Services

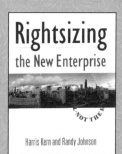

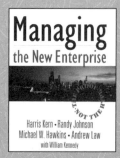

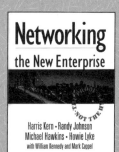

RIGHTSIZING THE NEW ENTERPRISE:
The Proof, Not the Hype
HARRIS KERN and RANDY JOHNSON

326 pages; ISBN 0-13-490384-6

The "how-to's" of rightsizing are defined in this detailed account based on the experiences of Sun Microsystems as it re-engineered its business to run on client/ server systems. This book covers rightsizing strategies and benefits, management and system administration processes and tools, and the issues involved in transitioning personnel from mainframe to UNIX support. RIGHTSIZING THE NEW ENTERPRISE presents you with proof that rightsizing can be done...and has been done.

MANAGING THE NEW ENTERPRISE:
The Proof, Not the Hype
HARRIS KERN, RANDY JOHNSON, MICHAEL HAWKINS, and ANDREW LAW, with WILLIAM KENNEDY

212 pages; ISBN 0-13-231184-4

MANAGING THE NEW ENTERPRISE describes how to build a solid technology foundation for the advanced networking and systems of the enterprise. Learn to re-engineer your traditional information technology (IT) systems while reducing costs! As the follow-up to RIGHTSIZING THE NEW ENTERPRISE, this volume is about relevant, critical solutions to issues challenging corporate computing in the 1990s and beyond.

TOPICS INCLUDE:

- Creating reliable UNIX distributed systems
- Building a production-quality enter-prise network
- Managing a decentralized system with centralized controls
- Selecting the right systems management tools and standards

NETWORKING THE NEW ENTERPRISE:
The Proof, Not the Hype
HARRIS KERN, RANDY JOHNSON, MICHAEL HAWKINS, and HOWIE LYKE, with WILLIAM KENNEDY and MARK CAPPEL

212 pages; ISBN 0-13-263427-9

NETWORKING THE NEW ENTERPRISE tackles the key information technology questions facing business professionals today—and provides real solutions. The book covers all aspects of network computing, including effective architecture, security, the Intranet, Web sites, and the resulting people issues culture shock.

OTHER NETWORKING TOPICS INCLUDE:

- Building a production quality network that supports distributed client/server computing
- Designing a reliable high-speed back-bone network
- Centralizing and controlling TCP/IP administration
- Evaluating and selecting key network components

Like RIGHTSIZING THE NEW ENTERPRISE and MANAGING THE NEW ENTERPRISE, its best-selling companion volumes, NETWORKING THE NEW ENTERPRISE is based on the authors' real-life experiences. It's the expert guide to every strategic networking decision you face. AND THAT'S NO HYPE.

...Also available from Sun Microsystems

CYBERCAREERS

MARY E. S. MORRIS and PAUL MASSIE

352 pages; ISBN 0-13-748872-6

Are you ready to cash in on the booming cyberspace job market? Internet experts Morris and Massie provide the kind of real-world guidance, hard-to-find information and practical advice you simply won't find anywhere else. Discover the skills you need to really compete for the most sought-after jobs in cyberspace. Learn how to plan for maximum success and how to plot a challenging and rewarding career path.

No matter what your background or experience, you will gain new insight into the dynamics of exciting new positions in a variety of industries on the cutting edge of the Internet and the World Wide Web. You will also learn from personal interviews with frontline professionals who are defining new careers.

UNIX BOOK OF GAMES

JANICE WINSOR

223 pages; ISBN 0-13-490079-2
(includes CD-ROM)

Put aside your work: it's time to play. THE UNIX BOOK OF GAMES brings together ten of the world's favorite games to keep you entertained: Flight Simulator, Go, Chess, Spider, Mahjongg, Reversi, Hearts, Canfield, Colossal Cave Adventure, and Klondike.

Every game comes with comprehensive rules, hints, lore, history, and complete installation instructions — or just play from the CD-ROM. The games come ready-to-play on Solaris and Linux, and the source code is provided if you want to compile it for a different version of UNIX.